a Bet —

OWNER'S MANUAL:

FOR BECOMING A SUCCESSFUL HUMAN BEING

P. A. ALEXANDER

KENDALL/HUNT PUBLISHING COMPANY
4050 Westmark Drive   Dubuque, Iowa 52002

CONTENTS

Being a Happy, Healthy Person
Definition of "Happy"
Exuding Inner Happiness

DEDICATION

To my parents, Pat and Dorothy, with all my love. I am so very grateful and happy that you were my parents. To Jose Silva, founder of the Silva Mind Control Method; without Jose I would not be on the path I am today. To Suzy Golin, my mentor and very dear friend, for helping me attain one of my greatest desires. To Frances Yarberry, my spiritual mentor and very dear friend, for her guidance along my spiritual path. To Jaimie Crytal Alexander, my best friend, for showing me, by example, that the past can be overcome and how to never give up. To Tommie S. Byers for always being there for me and you could always make me laugh, no matter the circumstances. To Dennis and Sheryl Devine, who thought that this book should be written and donated a computer and printer with love. To all my graduates that encouraged me, by reading this book before it was poublished. All of you have contributed to the success of this book. A Big **HUG** and **THANK YOU** to everyone.

Last, but not least, to all the wonderful people I have been fortunate enough to meet in my life and to those yet to come. Everyone, whether a good experience or not; I have learned a lesson from each one. Thank you for coming into my life. **You** have helped me to become a better person.

INTRODUCTION

The purpose of this book is to help you change your life in a positive and constructive manner. Your car comes with an owner's manual. Your TV comes with an owner's manual. In fact, everything we buy comes with an owner's manual. Why is it that as human beings, we did not come with an owner's manual?

I believe it is much more important that as human beings, we have a clear set of step-by-step instructions for assisting US in the process of changing our lives to make them better. We need to understand how to operate as a positive and constructive human being. But alas, we did not come with an owner's manual. We have had to manage on our own.

HOW WELL HAVE YOU DONE THUS FAR?

This book will cover nearly every area of your life. After all, we do not live at work, home, or school exclusively, twenty-four hours a day. Everyone DESERVES to have everything that we desire in life (as long as it hurts no one else).

Have fun with this book...Your life has been much too serious so far. Approach this book from the standpoint of having some exciting and great adventures. You can enjoy the process along the way. It isn't written "in stone" that changing must be a painful process. When you make a mistake, laugh at yourself. You will do better next time! Laughter truly is the best medicine! When you can learn to laugh at yourself, you have taken a giant leap forward in your development towards becoming a successful human being.

This is your User Friendly **"OWNER'S MANUAL"**. It is a book for beginners. This book was written to help CHILDREN AS WELL AS ADULTS who want to change their life but never knew how to do it. I suggest that you read the book completely to get an understanding of what is covered, and then go back and do the easy exercises.

It is my sincere hope, no matter your age, be that 12 or 120, that the following pages will help you change your life in a positive manner from this day forward. If you get one positive idea that helps you, I will have done my job in the writing of this book.

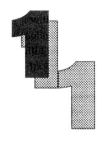

OVERVIEW

Everyone in the world wants to be successful! Successful in business, relationships, making money, self-improvement, love, happiness, school, and in about million others areas. The list can go on infinitely!

To begin with, ask yourself this question, "Exactly what is my definition of success?" For some, success is making a lot of money, getting a college degree, marriage, children, overcoming abuse and the addictions that accompany them. Whatever your definition of success, let us look at the dictionary's definition of success:

> *"A coming about, taking place or turning out to be as was hoped for; having a favorable result, as a successful mission; achieving or have achieved success; specifically have gained wealth, fame, rank, etc..."[1]*

How do we go about achieving success? I have read many books on certain aspects of improving my life but never the exact procedure on how to make this amazing transformation. I will share with you the process I have used, word-for-word, step-by-step.

How <u>you</u> achieve success depends on four things:

1. Time
2. Energy
3. Effort
4. Practice

How much time, energy, effort, and practice are you willing to put forth to effect your changes? Some changes will come very easily and quickly. Some changes may require more work. I do promise you this: these changes will come, but they are

---

[1]*Webster's New Twentieth Century Dictionary Unabridged*

dependent on the time, the energy, the effort, and the practice <u>you</u> are willing to give in making your changes.

I would like to share with you what I consider to be ten of the most important qualities to becoming a successful human being. The qualities are nothing new to you, and I know you are familiar with most of them, especially if you have read any self-development books.

My intention is to change your perspective about how you think of these qualities. How we perceive a particular concept or change determines the result. In other words, when we change our point of view or perspective, our end result changes.

The ten <u>qualities</u> of a successful human being are:

1. Self-Confidence
2. Self-Esteem
3. Positive Thinking
4. Goal Setting
5. Problem Solving
6. Relaxation
7. Stress Management
8. Health
9. Beliefs vs. Limiting Beliefs
10. Positive Imaging/Speaking

At this point, I have been asked by some adults, "How are the ten qualities of a successful human being going to help me make money?" Just bear with me; I will fully answer that question in a later chapter. I have also been asked this next question. "Is there any particular reason for the order in which you have listed the ten qualities?" Yes, there is a reason for the order in which I have selected the ten qualities. Before I answer that question, I would like to ask you a question.

How many times have you been talking to someone and not been able to get across what it is you were trying desperately to tell them? For some reason, that person just does not understand, no matter how many times you try to explain it? Or you think they understand, but to your amazement, they do just the opposite?

Perhaps it is because your definition of a word and their definition of the same word are entirely different! So that there are no similar misunderstandings occurring in this book, I will use Websters New Twenthieth Century Dictionary Unabridged for the concepts and the definitions of the words being used.

In Chapter Two, we will be discussing the first quality on my list: self-confidence. Beware, I am preparing to ask you **another** nosy question. I think that one of the best parts about reading a book, especially when the author asks you a question, (like the ones I will be asking you throughout this book), is that only you can hear the answer! Let's proceed to the next chapter on self-confidence.

SELF-CONFIDENCE

What is self-confidence, and how can I become more self-confident? (HERE is the "nosy question".) What is your definition of self-confidence? (No fair cheating by reading further and discovering what the dictionary says!)

In my research while working with many people, I have found their definition of self-confidence to be confused with their definition of self-esteem. So...the next question is, what is your definition of self-esteem? (Remember, no fair reading ahead).

Now that you have had time to think about both of these questions, do you consider self-confidence and self-esteem to have the same definition or a similar definition? Or, do you think they are entirely different?

So here we go, off to the dictionary, (I will give you a hint; they are entirely different). The dictionary's definition of self-confidence is:

"A reliance on one's own abilities, fortune or circumstances;
belief in one's own competency; self-reliance, assurance."

The dictionary's definition for self-esteem is:

"To set a value on, whether high or low."

In other words, how do you value or feel about yourself? Do you like yourself? Do you love yourself? (If you are like me, you wake up some mornings not quite sure how you feel about yourself!)

Think about someone **you** consider to be <u>successful</u>. Remember, leave money out of your consideration for the time being as we will discuss it in a later chapter. Do you agree that to be a successful person one must have a high self-confidence level and a high self-esteem level? Of course you do. This is why I have listed these two qualities first.

I believe the other eight qualities stem from the above. Each quality on my list has its own definition, but each quality depends on self-confidence and self-esteem to work properly. You may have a good self-confidence level without having a good self-esteem level or vice versa. The two definitions <u>are not interchangeable</u>. Self-confidence is a belief in one's abilities and talents. A good self-confidence level would be in knowing that you can tackle any job and do it well, such as:

1. typing the perfect letter
2. landscaping your yard better than a gardener
3. teaching your best friend math
4. you win (through determination) instead of the computer
5. opening your own business

How you feel about yourself (self-esteem) may have little to do with how well you perform your tasks. When no one is around to see you, you may feel as if you are the most unworthy person in the world, but this does not effect the performance of your job. You are <u>good</u> at what you do. In other words, you may be good in your profession without having a good self-esteem.

On the other hand, you may have a good self-esteem without being self-confident. Let me illustrate by telling you a story. I prefer using stories, as the majority of us can relate to and understand them. If you are of school age, change the stories to relate to your classroom situations.

All of us have known a person who sits in the office and does nothing but pound a typewriter or a computer eight hours a day, five days a week, fifty weeks a year. This person has a good self-esteem, but lacks the self-confidence in his or her abilities (for whatever reason) to be more than just a typist. This person, twenty years later, retires from this same position without ever having moved up in the company.

I believe most people want to be more than what they are today. They want to better themselves, but without self-confidence, they are never able to take the necessary risks to improve their situations.

There are exceptions to every rule, so for those of you who have held the same job for years or retired from that same job and were very happy with that job, I salute you. (But secretly, didn't you ever want to do something else?) I was never that fortunate. I get bored very easily. Once I learned my job, I wanted to move on and learn something new.

If I didn't have confidence in myself, I would never have undertaken the writing of this book. I was not a superior student in school. I made B's and C's. Yet, I know I have something to contribute to humanity by sharing what I have learned over many years.

As in any book, you will agree with hopefully the majority of the topics we are discussing. Others you might disagree with. That is perfectly all right! I do not expect you to agree with everything I say. All I ask is for you to keep an open mind.

Do not quickly reject material out-of-hand because it is new or presented from a different perspective. You will discover that the opinions you cling to depend on your point of view. Do more reading, attend seminars or lectures on the subject you are questioning, but always keep investigating. There are some excellent books on the market. I highly suggest reading The Silva Mind Control Method by Jose Silva. This is the course that helped me realize all the wonderful things I could do with my life and the only limitations I had were the ones I placed on myself.

To continue, put this information on your mental shelf for a while. If after your investigations the information does not feel comfortable to you and your belief system, (we will discuss beliefs in a later chapter) then discard the information. Keep nothing that does not help you become that successful person you want to be. Isn't that what we all want, to be the absolutely best person we can be and make it a better world to live in, so that when we depart this planet it will be better than when we arrived?

This process begins with developing the qualities of a successful person. All right, but how do I go about becoming self-confident and having a good self-esteem? The first step is thinking about what you want and what you can do to be more confident.

EXERCISE PROCEDURE

1. To start this process, find a quiet place where you can do your thinking.
2. Once you have discovered this haven, sit in a comfortable chair, (I do not suggest lying down as the body is trained to believe you are going to sleep), and close your eyes. If there is anyone else in the house tell them you need some quiet time and not to disturb you until you open the door. The reason I ask you to close your eyes is that in the beginning you will find that you are easily distracted by things going on around you. A quiet place means no TV or radio, (sorry, kids). Another reason is that scientists have said that eighty percent of your sensory input comes in through your eyes and tends to keep you from concentrating on why you are there in the first place. You must learn to concentrate on what you are thinking.
3. Now that your eyes are closed, take several deep breaths. (Deep breathing helps relax the body so you can learn to concentrate on your thoughts, not the tightness in your neck or shoulders.) Inhale to a slow count of eight; hold for a slow count of four, then exhale slowly to a slow count of eight. Do this several times until you feel your body relaxing. Concentrate only on your breathing and feeling your body relaxing. If you find your mind is wandering, this is all right; it happens to all of us in the beginning. Bring your thoughts back to breathing and relaxing. How many breaths you take is up to you. I recommend at least 5 deep breaths. When you feel relaxed, continue with the next step.

4. I want you to imagine a room, any room you wish. This room will be called the "Situation Room". This room needs to be a place where you feel completely safe, comfortable and relaxed. This is one of the rooms where you will be doing your mental work.

This room will be the first of two rooms that leads to your "GOAL ROOM". In this room, you are going to examine the situation/problem as it is at this moment.

5. When you are in the "Situation Room" see yourself in a particular situation when you were not as confident as you would like to have been. Remember who was there, the conversation, how the surroundings looked, how you acted, how others reacted to you, and especially important, how you felt. Remember as many details as possible.

If you need to write all of the above down on paper before beginning this exercise, please do so.

6. After you have remembered everything you can, create a door that leads you into your second room, the "Rehearsal Room". Walk through this door into your "Rehearsal Room". You will make believe that you are watching yourself, imagining how you would have liked the previous situation to have occurred. Decide how you should have acted, what you should have said, and how you would have felt if things would have gone the way you wanted them to.

It is most important that you see yourself making the right choices for a successful conclusion!

7. Now create another door. Walk through this door into your "Goal Room", and visualize or imagine yourself actually being in this room as you did in your "Rehearsal Room". We are feeling our emotions right now. We are carrying on the conversation right now. We can actually touch an object and feel the hardness or softness of it, right now. If someone were wearing cologne, we could smell it right now! It is the same as if you were remembering a walk on the beach when you were on vacation. You are there again to smell the salt air, hear the waves crashing on the shore, looking up to see the clouds, feeling the sand under your feet. This is what you do in the third room.

In the first two rooms, we were **dissociating** (like we were watching a movie). In this third room, we are **associating** because we are actually there living the experience that we created in the second room.

Let me share with you a story about myself. I had a bad problem with self-confidence. When I was growing up, I was always being compared with the other children in the neighborhood. "Why can't you be like Cathy, or Fran, or Sylvia?" (Does this sound familiar?) It seemed like I was never pretty enough or smart enough, etc. I was basically a shy person. So as an adult, after years of being told I was not good enough, I believed it.

At the age of twenty-five, I decided I was tired of not being **good enough**. I decided to do something about it. I chose to change into the person I wanted to be.

This is the procedure I followed to change my self-confidence. I observed other people I thought were self-confident. I selected a trait I would like to have as a part of me. I decided that the **ultimate act of self-confidence was being able to walk up to someone and to be the first to extend my hand to introduce myself.**

I was the proverbial wallflower. I remembered how shy I was, always standing in the corner, and never initiating a conversation. When I was spoken to, I said only what I had to say because I did not think that **what I had to say** was important. I had the feeling of being totally alone. I wanted to be included, but I did not know how to go about being included and **feeling comfortable with it**.

I practiced four or five times a day with the above exercise until I felt very comfortable with the idea of walking up to someone and introducing myself first. The next step was to try it out in the real world. The following is what I did:

> I was invited to a football party at someone's home. (One of those bring-a-dish affairs.) On the way to the house, I kept practicing my self-confidence exercise in the car so I would be ready. When I arrived, I went to the front door and rang the bell. When the host answered the door, I discovered that my shoulders were slumping and that I was looking at the floor so as not to see who was there. I made my way to the buffet table to set down my dish. I found myself, out of habit, heading for a corner away from everyone. I started to sit down, and about halfway in the squatting position, I jumped up as if someone had "goosed" me. At this point, my silent self said, "This is not why you came to this party. Walk over to that group of people and introduce yourself." But I said to myself, "I am frightened, I can hardly breathe, and I think I am frozen to the floor." My silent voice replied, "You can do it. Remember how you felt when you were practicing. Take a deep breath and move your right foot forward. Now take another deep breath and move your left foot forward."

Let me tell you, I felt as if my legs were stuck in mud up to my hips. Luckily, I only had about six feet to cover. By the time I got there, I was exhausted.

I had been raised that it is not polite to interrupt anyone's conversation, so I stood there very patiently waiting for an opportunity to speak. As their conversation wound down, they started to separate and leave the area. I thought I had a reprieve from actually having to initiate a conversation when the person nearest me turned around and almost "ran over" me. Startled, I put this silly grin on my face, immediately stuck out my hand, and said, "Hello, my name is Patricia. What is your name?" We chatted for a moment; then they went their way, and I happily went mine. I instantly found a chair and sat down.

I had to sit down. My legs would no longer support me! Mentally and physically, I was spent, but I was elated emotionally. I had actually done it! I remember nothing else about that evening, but I will always remember that experience. Each time I would take the initiative, it became easier and easier.

The most important part to remember is that when you have made a positive change a part of you, choose another goal to put in its place. Keep making your changes until you are the person you envision. This is what I did to become the person I am today. This is what I do every day. I practice becoming what I want to be tomorrow. I know change can be frightening, but remember how you are going to feel when you have made that change. Now I wonder why I was ever afraid.

Can you tell me the answer to why I finally became comfortable and never thought about being afraid ever again? Sure you can. It is because of the practice time I put into becoming comfortable with my change. I made it a <u>habit</u>.

Let me share a little secret with you. There are many others out there who are less confident than you. I promise. It is just that some people have a better mask or front, so their lack of self-confidence <u>does not appear to show.</u>

What is happening during your practice sessions? You are becoming an actor or actress. Isn't this what actors do when rehearsing for a part? How well they rehearse or take on their part is what makes us, the audience, believe in the characters they are portraying. Now apply this analogy to yourself. If you put in only a few hours of rehearsal (or practice time) a week, how believable are you going to be?

Actors have a saying: "Fake it 'till you make it!" This is exactly what you will be doing, faking it until you make it! The more practice you put in using your "Goal Room" exercise, the more quickly you will achieve your desired end result. Remember, some of the changes you want to make in your life will come quickly and easily; others may not.

When you spend time, energy, effort and practice into making a particular change and find it is not becoming a comfortable part of you or for you, then release and erase your mental image you have created in your "Goal Room".

Not everything will become part of you. Remember, that is **all right**. I know you want <u>everything</u> to work for you - so did I. You have not FAILED! The change you want to make right now may not be right for you at this time.

This could be due to several factors, such as your present knowledge, growth, wisdom, etc.. I know, you wanted this to happen thirty minutes ago! All of us are impatient in one area or another. **It will come**. I am sure there are other changes you would like to make. You can always come back to this particular change later in your life. Move on with your life, and continue to make your changes. You will discover that with each success your confidence will grow.

There is something else I would like to share with you at this time. Do not fall into the trap of measuring your successes. For instance, "this is only a little success." A success is a success. It reminds me of hearing someone say, "She is only a little bit pregnant." How can one be just a little bit pregnant? You either are or you are not. You are either successful or you are not! Where is it written that success must be measured, and who gave us the measuring stick? What YOU might consider to be a small or partial success might be a GIGANTIC success to someone else. Let's get out of the habit of measuring NOW. If you need to, re-read this paragraph again.

If you prefer to measure your success, by all means go ahead, but I believe that this is a way to make yourself feel as if you have failed, AND it may tend to inhibit you in the future. Most people will think, "Well, if this is a partial success, then I must have failed!" NO, NO, NO, NO, NO! You have successfully completed part of whatever it was you wanted to do. Now you need to re-think the rest of whatever it was you were doing to discover the errors. Remember, you are a human being and allowed to make mistakes or errors.

You are now taking control of your life and deciding in which direction YOU want your life to proceed. Once you start taking control of your life, never again will you allow someone to control you. The only person you are responsible for in this lifetime is you. (Oh no, I can hear parents already saying, "But I am responsible for my children"). Remember, this is a book about self, not your responsibilities to others.

Only you can decide to make your life better. The previous pages are the beginning of this process for making your life happier and more rewarding.

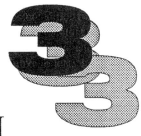

SELF-ESTEEM

Do you remember the definition of self-esteem? Self-esteem is:

"to set a value on, whether high or low."

In other words, do you like yourself or do you love yourself? Exactly how do you feel about yourself?

What is in your set of beliefs, about yourself, that keeps your esteem low? Perhaps one of the following statements were repeatedly said to you when you were a child:

1. You are so stupid. Can't you do anything right?
2. If you don't go to college, you will never amount to anything!
3. You would be so pretty...if you would only lose weight!
4. A woman's place is in the home.
5. You are an accident looking for a place to happen!
6. You were a mistake at birth.
7. Why can't you get a better paying job?
8. Why didn't you make the cheerleading/drill team?
9. Why didn't you make the football team?
10. You can't even do anything simple!

Have you heard any of those, or perhaps thousands just like them? There are many more I can add to the list, but I think you get the idea.

Let's stop right now and examine what has been said to you. Did you believe it? Whoever it was that made the statement, are they perfect and all knowing? Do they ever make mistakes? What was their motive or reason for making the statement? What was their intent in making the statement? Does it really matter why? (As far as I know, there was only one perfect person on this planet, depending on your beliefs.) The only reason we need to remember these statements is so we can use them to help us make our changes.

Let's choose the first example, and we will practice using our "Goal Room" exercise. Before you close your eyes, remember when was the first time you heard that statement being said to you, your age, the circumstances surrounding the incident, how you felt, what, if anything, you said? How many times was the statement repeated? How many times have you said this statement to yourself, saying it before anyone else could or made a joke about how stupid you were?

WARNING, WARNING! Here comes another **nosy** question. Are you perfect or are you a human being? I believe most of you said the latter. If you said the former, this book isn't for you. If you said "human being", then as a human being, we are allowed to make mistakes or errors. This does not mean you are a bad person. This does not mean that you are "less than" or "not as good as" anyone else. All it means is that at that particular time, you were not paying as much attention as you should have to whatever it was you were doing and made a mistake. This does not make you stupid. All it shows is a lack of concentration and focus on your part. How can we correct this feeling we have of being stupid? By practicing our mental exercise and allowing ourselves to be human.

EXERCISE FOR SELF-ESTEEM/SELF-CONFIDENCE

1. Close your eyes and take several deep breaths, feeling your body relaxing with each breath.
2. In the "Situation Room" remember when you were told that you were stupid; feel your emotions; remember what you doing, what you were thinking, how stupid you were feeling.
3. Go through the door into your "Rehearsal Room". See yourself responding to the same situation and telling the person that you made a mistake, due to the lack of attention on your part. Apologize and state that you will make every effort to do better. Include all the emotions that go with the above situation. (Remember, you are watching yourself as if you are on TV).
4. Go through the door into your "Goal Room". You are actually in the room, with the person in front of you. Feel the experience when you tell them you made a mistake and will make every effort in the future to do better. Hear them reply to you that we all make mistakes and that you are a smart, intelligent person, and they know you will do better.

Do this exercise over and over again until you fully believe it. Say aloud, several times a day, "I am a smart and intelligent human being." You are what you think.

Perhaps if you have feelings of low self-esteem, they may be very deeply rooted. In this case, if it is financially possible, seek out a good therapist who has dealt with the same kinds of problems with which you need to deal. A good therapist can help you discover what is causing your poor self-image, which in turn will help you put into effect the changes you want in your life. When you discover the cause, then use your "Goal Room" exercise to help you make the changes!

There are other choices you might prefer. There are many excellent self-development books on the market that I highly recommend. These are just a few:

1. The Silva Mind Control Method--Jose Silva
2. John Bradshaw: On the Family--John Bradshaw
3. What to Say When You Talk to Yourself--Dr. Shad Helmstetter, Phd.
4. Love is Letting Go of Fear--Gerald Jampolsky, M.D.
5. Living in the Light--Shakti Gawain
6. TOXIC PARENTS: Overcoming their hurtful legacy and reclaiming your life--Dr. Susan Forward
7. Key to Yourself--Venice Bloodworth
8. You Will See It, When You Believe It--Dr. Wayne Dyer
9. You Can Heal Your Life--Louise Hay
10. The Celestine Prophecy--James Redfield
11. The Force--Stuart Wilde

There are also some excellent seminars that will help you. I stumbled upon The Silva Mind Control Method quite by accident. It was through this particular course that I changed my life forever. I would not be able to write this book and to share with you the contents of this book were it not for the Silva course. Dr. Shad Helmstetter has Self-Talk seminars which help you to understand and change the way you talk to yourself. Louise Hay has several seminars covering a variety of different topics, from self-imaging to health. The other authors I have mentioned above also have seminars. Just remember to investigate all new information which comes into your life. Trust your intuition and common sense. Everything that is out there may not be right for you at this time. Continue with your investigations to improve your knowledge.

When your self-esteem rises, your self-confidence level will rise also. When you feel better about yourself, you are willing to take more risks in other areas. For example, you will introduce yourself to others **first**. Soon, when you make a mistake, you will not take it as a reflection on your character. You will say, "I am all right. I just wasn't paying attention. I let my mind wander; I will do better next time."

Yes, you will achieve this attitude. I found that when my confidence rose, so did my esteem, and vice versa.

Make every effort to stay away from the people who have caused your low self-esteem. They weren't helping you, but damaging you. Misery loves company! Soon you will notice that THEY have a self-esteem or self-confidence problem of their own. When you start feeling better about yourself, they seem to disappear from your life.

This attrition will happen naturally. Why? Because they are not able to bring you "down to their level" anymore. Ever hear the saying, "Birds of a feather flock together?" Make new friends who will help you realize your self-worth and value you for who and what you are. Associate with positive thinkers!

This process can happen quickly or take forever. Be honest. What kind of excuse will you give yourself this time? Look at your desire to change. Did you really put in the practice time you should have to make your dream come true? **Did you really believe that it would happen?** Was this goal something you wanted so badly you could taste it? That is what it takes to make it happen!

PERSEVERANCE and DETERMINATION

An example for the younger folks reading this book:
Remember when you wanted to do something a lot? For some reason or other your parents did not want you to do it. Did you give up or did you keep giving good reasons why you should be allowed to do it? You did not give up! That is perseverance and determination.

My self-esteem and self-confidence were once so low, I felt that when I looked up, I could see a "snake's belly". Why did I feel this way? Because I was always being compared to the girl next door or the one down the street. I grew up feeling that I was never good enough.

I also thought it was my job to please everyone, no matter the cost to myself. When you grow up with a lack of good self-esteem and self-confidence you think the only way to be accepted is to please people. When you are a child, this is especially true. Our parents have certain expectations of us. We learn at an early age how to control and manipulate others by pleasing them to attain whatever we want.

As we grow older we sometimes sacrifice what we know to be the "right" thing to do by taking short cuts which require the "pleasing" of others to reach a goal we have in mind, thinking that we could possibly not reach that goal as quickly or possibly not reach it at all if we don't take this short cut.

Let me pass on a bit of experience. People know when you are using this tactic to attain your own ends. You immediately lose not only your self-respect but that of others as well.

As an adult, you have to please no one but yourself. You can choose to let the past keep on affecting you, or you can choose to change. How can you please anyone else if you are not pleased with yourself?

But, how about pleasing your boss, spouse, parents, grandparents etc? Let me ask you a question. Are you confusing the word "please" with the word "responsibility"? Again I say, this is a book about self and creating the self that we want to be, not about responsibilities we need to fulfill for others such as what is required from us in the work place or at school. How can we fulfill these responsibilities to others if we are not able to fulfill responsibilities to ourselves? Do not confuse being pleased with self with fulfilling the responsibilities or duties we have to others. Yes, you can do things to please others if you choose to, but not at the expense of your own happiness or accomplishing a goal through manipulation.

14

I was so determined to change that I let <u>nothing</u> get in my way. I wanted desperately to be like everyone else instead of the "patsy" I had been all my life.

It has been a long process for me, but I would not go back to the way I was for anything in this world. I work every day on the changes I want to make in my life. I know that if I had a book like this one and followed its insights and advice, I would be farther along in my self-development than I am today.

In 1971, when I took the Silva course, there were relatively few self-development books or self-help groups. There were fewer therapists. I worked a lot by trial and error, but I never gave up. I have been told that I am very stubborn. I do not agree with that statement. I am very **determined!** There is a definite difference between the two words. The dictionary's definition of stubborn is:

> *"refusing to yield, obey, or comply; resisting doggedly; determined; obstinate...hard to handle, treat, or deal with; intractable."*

The dictionary's definition of determined is:

> *"having one's mind made up; decided; resolved; resolute; unwavering."*

How determined are you?

Make up your mind now that "nothing" or "no one" will deter you from becoming the person you want to be. You can have the same results as I have had or even better. I am no one special. I am just like you. I have average intelligence. I am working on becoming a better human being today, and becoming much better than I was yesterday.

I have confidence in you and your desire to be all that you can be. I know you can and will achieve <u>your</u> desired end results, which are the positive changes you want to manifest in your life.

POSITIVE THINKING

Ask anyone if they think they are positive thinkers, and most people will say yes. But, exactly what is positive thinking? The best definition I have ever read or heard is

"Visualizing or imagining your desired end result."

Ok, you understand that definition, but what is the definition of visualization and imagination? When I have asked people their definitions, they think that the definitions are the same or similar.

What is your definition? (Remember, no reading ahead for my definition.) Visualization is very misleading. It is not about seeing only. Visualization involves using all your senses, including your **mind**. The dictionary's definition is:

"... anything visualized; a mental picture."

In other words, visualizing is anything you have seen, heard, tasted, touched, smelled, what you have thought, and what you have felt.

Visualization is your memory.

But, you thought that was also the definition of imagination. This is the dictionary's definition of imagination:

"... the act or power of creating mental images of what has never been actually experienced ..."

So, what is imagination? Imagination is just the opposite of visualization. Imagination is that which you have never experienced through your five senses, what you have thought, or what you have felt.

Imagination is creativity.

How do you use this with positive thinking? Recall the definition of positive thinking. Positive thinking is visualizing or imagining your desired end result. Haven't we been using positive thinking in our last two exercises? We human beings think in mental images, not words or symbols like a computer.

Your thoughts are energy. You are an "energy being" (made of energy) with physical matter (your skin) surrounding your energy. We know from science that energy flows in a circle. Your thoughts, directed by your mind, lead you in the direction you choose to go. But which direction are you going?

Are you going in a **positive** direction or a negative direction? Do you usually attain the things you want in life? Does opportunity beat down your door? Does everything you touch turn to gold?

Or do you keep attracting negative people, situations, and things into your life? Have you ever wondered why God or the Universe has decided to pick on you? I am here to tell you, God or the Universe did not pick you out specifically to make your life miserable! You have done that to yourself, perhaps with the help of your thoughts, parents, teachers, preachers, friends and others.

I know that is a very strong statement to make. Look into your past. When were you ever taught to think, speak, or act in a positive manner? When you said something negative, were you encouraged to think positively and improve your attitude? Or did people agree with you and add more negativity to what you had said? You should have been corrected, on the spot, with the positive way to rephrase what you had said to help you learn to think and speak in a positive manner. So, in essence, what we often have are negative attitudes and we learn negative thinking which cause failure.

Why is it that successful people always seem to attract the wonderful things in life? It is due to the way they think. It is due to their expectations. Unlike the majority of us, they do not think of all the things that can go wrong. They think of all the things that can go right! Have you ever heard this saying, "What goes around, comes around"? Or perhaps this one, "What ye sow, so shall ye reap"? Both statements are referring to the energy you send out into the Universe and what you expect to come back to you. **Expect** the best, and you will **receive** the best!

Would you consider the following a good example of positive thinking? This is a portion of a story about Thomas Edison I heard years ago.

> For years, Edison had tried several methods to create a successful filament for the light bulb. His idea was that electricity was a safer, cleaner alternative for lighting. The glass globe was the easy part, but every filament he tried would burn out. Despite others saying it was impossible, that he was a failure, he kept at his task until he discovered the filament that worked! He **knew** he could do it.
>
> Would you like to know his response to all the negative statements made to him? He said, "No, I am not a failure. I am

only a failure if I repeat one of those experiments that I know does not work." He would not allow others to affect his thinking.

How often have you repeated a mistake? How often have you "reacted", instead of "acted"? This is an example of repeating a mistake.

Have you ever used a vacuum cleaner to sweep your carpet? As you are sweeping the carpet, did you ever sweep over an item the vacuum cleaner would not pick up? What did you do? You swept over the item again, hoping this time the vacuum cleaner would pick it up. As you watch, the item appears on the carpet as if it were glued in place. What did you do? You reached down, picked up the item to make sure it wasn't glued to the floor, looked it over very carefully and put it back on the floor to give the vacuum cleaner ONE MORE CHANCE to do its' job.

I hope each of you recognized yourself in the above story and had a good laugh. But wouldn't you call what we did, when we went over the item several times, repeating a mistake? This seems like a trivial story. Think about your behavior.

If energy flows in a circle and what goes around comes around, what happens if you send out **positive** energy/thoughts? If you send out negative energy/thoughts, what comes back to you? Now ask yourself this question, "What have I been attracting to me by my thoughts?"

You have to learn how to control and be aware of what you are thinking at all times. Remember: You are what you think about. How you have thought in the past will affect the kind of life you have at the present time. The past is a good predictor of the future.

What can you do to become more aware of your thoughts? You should learn to focus and concentrate. Pay attention to your every thought. You know that your thoughts are energy, and they will come back to you. Practicing everyday with the exercises in this book will help you to concentrate. But you are the one who must make the time, expend the energy, put forth the effort, and practice. Make it a habit!

How many days does it take to form a habit? It takes 21 days to form a habit. Scientists have finally been able to see into the brain and determine why it takes 21 days to form a habit. Would you like to know how it happens?

Between the neurons in the brain are the synapses. When a thought comes along, the synapse forms a bridge so the information can be passed from one neuron to the next neuron. When the information has passed over a synaptic bridge, the synapse disappears until more information of the same kind needs to be sent again. When the same information is passed over a 21 day period, the synapse hardens and becomes a permanent bridge. This is how a habit is formed.

How do we dispose of a bad habit? By forming a new, and better habit to replace the old one. When the old one is no longer reinforced, the synaptic bridge softens again and goes back to its original state.

Did you realize that all we consist of is learned habits? You have chosen to be either this, or that. You have repeated the action over and over again until you made it a habit, or what some people call "second nature". I do not want to break anyone's bubble here, but you were not born that way. Your CHOSE to be the way you are.

My favorite example is when I hear someone say, "That is just the way I am." This is the worst excuse I have ever heard for staying the way you are. What I really hear is, "I am comfortable with the way I am", or "I do not know how to change this about myself and this is the only excuse I can give for staying this way," "or I am too lazy," or "it takes too much time to change."

It is up to you to change those habits which are keeping you from being all you can be. Send out positive energy so you can receive what you deserve to have in life. Here is a story to illustrate what I mean.

Many people, when they are ready to go to sleep at night, start thinking about what has happened to them during the day. I like to compare it to carrying a piece of mental luggage around with us. In this mental luggage, we put in everything that has happened for that particular day. As we are about to go to sleep, we put that piece of mental luggage on our tummies. We open up the luggage and review those events.

What is it that we review? Is it all the good or positive events, or is it all the negative events? For example:

1. To start off our day, we woke up late.
2. The kids gave us trouble getting ready.
3. The boss was waiting at our desk, looking at his watch.
4. Your big contract did not close.
5. The computer was down for six hours.

and so on, ad infinitum! Be honest; it is the negative things we go over and over again in our minds! No wonder your boss is always grumpy. You are the one sending out the negative energy. You are the one expecting him to be this way. So what have you received? Why are you surprised when you get exactly what you were thinking?

You know now that thoughts are energy and energy flows in a circle. What have you been sending out, and what can you expect to come back to you? Ask yourself now, "What have I normally been thinking about just before I go to sleep?" Do you understand how **YOU** have created your life? By your thoughts, whatever you think <u>will come back to you</u>. I always thought that people picked on me. Guess what people did? I thought it, believed it, came to expect it, and that is what I received.

It is extremely important to be aware of and to guard what you are thinking because, my friends, your thoughts will, and do, come back to you. They come back to you larger than what you sent out originally because your thoughts have attracted to them what they are; negative thoughts attracting <u>more</u> negative energy. The same occurs with your positive thoughts.

This is why some people seem to receive everything they want in life. They always think of their <u>desired end result</u>. They are always <u>aware</u> of their thoughts and are always <u>in control</u> of what they are thinking. Nothing or no one stops them from their goals. Be determined (not stubborn) to achieve whatever goals you set for yourself.

SETTING GOALS

I don't know about you, but every time I hear something like, "You need to learn how to set goals," it's as if someone is running their fingernails down a chalkboard! In the past that is all I have heard. Never once, after having gone to a goal-setting seminar, had I ever come out knowing what to do about setting goals. In fact, I came out more confused than when I went in!

Several hundred dollars later, after having bought all the products that went along with the seminar, I would look at them and say, "Now what do I do with all this stuff?" No one ever showed me a simple, easy, and effective way to set goals, much less, an effective way to use them.

I believe in doing things that are fast, easy, and effective. Let me share with you a way that works. I promise (and I do not make promises lightly), that if you follow what I am going to show you, you will attain your goals, faster and easier than ever before.

GOAL SETTING IN FOUR STEPS

STEP ONE

1. Find a quiet place (not 5 minutes stolen
   at lunch time somewhere), preferably at home.
2. Close your eyes and take several deep breaths to
   relax the body and mind.
3. Ask yourself, "What do I want?"

That sounds easy enough, doesn't it? But instead, I have discovered from my previous experiences of asking people what they **DO** want in life that I usually receive answers from them stating what it is they **DO NOT** want in life. For example:

1. I don't want to be a secretary all my life.
2. I don't want to be broke all the time.
3. I don't want to live in an apartment forever.

Phew! Ok, I will ask you again, "What DO you want in life?" You have told me what you do not want; now tell me what you do want. I get total silence and blank

23

looks on their faces. We have been conditioned all our lives to think negatively. We do not know how to respond in a positive manner to a question.

All right, let's begin again and think about what we <u>do</u> want in our personal and business/school lives. We need two categories because we usually want different things for each one. Below are some examples of what you might want:

1. I want to live in my own home.
2. I want to advance to a higher position at work.
3. I want to make the cheerleading team.
4. I want to be healthy.

Which of the above are personal goals? Which are business goals?

<u>STEP TWO</u>

1. Open your eyes.
2. Go get a piece of paper and a pen/pencil.
3. Write your goals down.

It is very important to write your goals down. Have you ever noticed that when you keep your goals in your mind, that is where they stay. The majority of your goals are never accomplished.

Why? The reason is you have not formed a habit. Remember when we talked about neurons and the synaptic bridges? <u>Your goals must be said in the exact same words every time.</u> When you think a goal, one neuron is impressed. When you say it out loud, another neuron is impressed. When you hear it, another neuron is impressed.

Personally, I do not like the word "goal". I prefer to think of a goal as a "destination" (but you choose which word you like). This is some place I want to be, rather than where I am. I know you have noticed that life is a journey, with many stops along the way. There is never a final destination except when we depart this planet. Your goals are your stops along the way. Enjoy your journey through life by planning with your goals whatever you would like to HAVE-BE-or-DO. You deserve whatever you wish. There is abundance for everyone in this Universe. All you need to do is take control and ask the Universe for want you want.

On your sheet of paper at the top of the page on the left side, write your Personal Goals. On the top of the page at the right side, write your Business/School Goals. Underneath these headings write short-term, medium-term and long-term goals. Short term goals, are ones that should be reached in one week to a month. Medium term goals should be reached in three to six months. Long term goals should be reached within one year. You can make your goals any length of time you wish. Do whatever is comfortable for you, time-wise. List five goals under each subheading. Your goal sheet should look like this:

24

PERSONAL GOALS	BUSINESS/SCHOOL GOALS
Short Term	**Short Term**
1.	1.
2.	2.
3.	3.
4.	4.
5.	5.
Medium Term	**Medium Term**
1.	1.
2.	2.
3.	3.
4.	4.
5.	5.
Long Term	**Long Term**
1.	1.
2.	2.
3.	3.
4.	4.
5.	5.

(Excuse me for a moment; a small, four-legged interruption! Cleopatra, my cat, insists on petting. She has me well trained!) That did not take long, did it? Oh yes, back to where we were. At this time, you should have thirty goals listed. Fifteen personal goals and fifteen business/school goals. Be careful to keep your personal goals and business/school goals as separate as possible. I know that some may cross over, but decide into which column the goal should go. As you accomplish one goal, put another in it's place. Remember, we change every day. Make sure the change you receive is the change you want.

STEP THREE
1. Wording your goals.
2. Re-write your goals now with the proper wording.

The proper wording is the next to the most important step. Start your goals with the two most important words in your vocabulary. Would you like to guess what they are?

I AM.

Stop and think about it. When you say "I Am", you are stating a **belief** about yourself. You say "I am" this, or "I am" that. Think about one of the previous examples when someone said, "This is just the way I am." You do not have to stay the way you are if YOU decide to change it.

Make sure each of your goal sentences begin with the words, "I am". Each sentence should be four to five words long. You have thirty goals to read. If you were to write a paragraph on each one, (let's be honest here) how many times do you think you would read them out loud?

Here are some examples of the proper phrasing. If you are unhealthy, what do you want? Health, of course! So how would you state that as a goal? This should only take three words. I am healthy. But the sentence is not complete. We left the most important word out. What in the world could that possibly be? I know several people that are in general good health, yet they have health problems. Can one have a broken arm and still be in good health? So how do we rephrase our goal statement? I am in perfect health. After all, isn't that what we want? Suppose you are unemployed? What do you want, starting your sentence with "I am"? I am employed. Again, we have left out a key word. If you are worth $50.00 an hour, do you want to work for $3.65 an hour? This is what you would say. I am profitably employed.

I hope at this point you are beginning to realize that you must say exactly what you mean, and mean exactly what you say. The Universe has a strange sense of humor. Believe me, you get exactly what you ask for. (I knew you knew that!)

Have you noticed what verb tense I am using? Is it past, present, or future tense? Present tense, of course. If we phase in the future with:

1. I will
2. I am going to,

this is exactly where your goals are going to stay, in the future. If we phrase in the past:

1. I should have
2. I was going to
3. I possibly could have,

How can you change what already has happened? The past is gone. We have no control over what was. The only control we have is in the present. What we control in the present affects the results we will have in the future.

But, how can you say you are in perfect health when you are not in good health right now?

Several publications, such as Prevention Magazine and The Mind/Brain publication, along with several renowned scientists, many belonging to the Mind Institute in California, have done extensive research about the power of the mind over our bodies. When you keep repeating every day that you are in perfect health, your body will start responding to that command. (Remember to use visualization to see yourself in perfect health.) You are what you think!

26

How many times have you told people how bad your health is? How many times have you thought it? Then to undo what you have already done, you must create a new habit, or set of instructions, for the body to follow. The more often you say or think it, the more quickly the body will start mending itself. Soon, the old instructions to the brain will weaken. The synaptic bridge will disappear and the body will start manifesting perfect health.

This may take some time, depending on your state of health. In my case it took several years. I had bleeding ulcers, thirty percent nerve damage in my neck, (due to several car accidents) which produced excruciating pain, lower back problems (also due to car accidents) obesity, headaches, and chronic bronchitis. Are you getting the idea? In other words, I was a physical wreck. I was determined to change my state of health, and I did.

Today I am in perfect health (as far as I know) with none of the problems I had in the past. I know now that my thoughts had greatly contributed to every physical problem I had. (Hey, sickness or bad health is an excellent way to get sympathetic attention, right?) Is this kind of attention negative or positive reinforcement?

OK, you understand about health problems, but how is that going to help you get a job? What are your thoughts about getting a job? Your thoughts are energy, remember? Are you sending out the positive energy to attract to you the kind of job you want?

This doesn't mean that you sit on your backside, with a silver platter in both hands, waiting for the job to come to you! You send out resumes, check the newspaper, go on interviews, and most important of all is to talk to friends about what kind of job you are looking for. Word of mouth is always the best advertiser.

There is a saying from a very famous book: "Ask, and ye shall receive." How do you expect to receive if you don't ask? Don't expect the Universe to read your mind! You must tell the Universe what you want. You do this with your thoughts.

I would love to be with you when you find yourself in the "right place at the right time". I am sure the look on your face would be priceless. Remember, your thoughts have put you in the "right place at the right time". If you are not in the "right place at the right time", how have you been thinking?

This might be a goal you would like to have on your goal list. I am always in the right place at the right time. Another famous saying is, "The Universe/God helps those who help themselves." You are now learning to help yourself, by asking the Universe for the abundance that is your birthright. There is abundance for everyone. Allow yourself to take your share of that abundance.

STEP FOUR
1. Read your goals out loud
2. Read them out loud at least twice a day

This is the most important step of all. The best times to read your goals aloud are in the morning when you first get up and before you go to sleep at night. Every goal setting seminar I have attended agrees with this.

Gee, Patricia, I don't have any extra time in the mornings, and I am just too pooped at night. Where can I find the extra time?

Would you like a fast, easy, and effective way to read them in the morning and at night without having to make any extra time for it? Where is the first place you go in the morning when you get out of bed, (excluding coffee) and where is the last place you go before going to bed? EXACTLY! The bathroom! (I knew you knew this one too!)

I want you to get your goal sheet and put a piece of Scotch tape across the top. Take the goal sheet and tape it to your bathroom mirror.

"Why the bathroom, Patricia, of all places?" Ladies, where do you put on your make-up, take a bath, and do your finishing touches before you leave the house? Guys, where do you take a shower and shave? The point to all of this is, why not do something constructive and positive with your time to help you achieve what you want in life? (since you have to be in there anyway!).

Let's put out the positive energy in the mornings to attract to us what we want. At night, instead of reviewing what went wrong during the day, again let's send out the positive energy to make the next day what we want it to be. The only reason we need to review the things that did not go as we would have wanted is to correct them.

YOU CAN USE YOUR "GOAL ROOM" EXERCISE WITH EACH ONE OF YOUR GOALS.

You will achieve your goals even faster with this procedure.

You do not have to believe in anything I have said, but if you want to see your life change in the direction YOU want, just do it!

Make it a habit to say your goals out loud, every day. When your goals start to happen, just the way you have asked for them to happen, then you will believe. When you start believing, they will happen faster than before. Practice with your goals for twenty-one days, and you will see the "fruits of your labor". Then, just like I did, you will wonder why you did not do it sooner. I wish I could save you wasted time, but I realize you have to do it and see the results for yourself, just as I did.

Your goals are your destiny. There are many paths you can take. Keep your goals in mind. Keep a copy of your goals in your billfold or purse. Review them several times a day. Soon opportunity will be beating down your door instead of passing you by, (as perhaps it has done in the past). When opportunity does knock, no matter how lightly, you will be listening, ready to take action.

Lastly, **EXPECT** your goals to happen. Accept and believe that the Universe is working on your behalf. You have asked and now you are waiting on delivery.

28

A reminder: Keep your goal sentences as short as possible. Say exactly what you mean, and mean exactly what you say. (We will go into "saying exactly what you mean and meaning exactly what you say" in more depth in a later chapter). Make your goals a habit. Don't put them off. What happens when you procrastinate? Do it **NOW**! I rest my case!

PROBLEM SOLVING

What is the definition of the word "Problem"? The dictionary defines it as:

"a question proposed for solution; hence a perplexing question, situation or person."

When you hear the word "problem", does it have a **negative OR emotional** context for you? For instance, someone comes up to you and in a very agitated or excited voice says, "I have a problem!" What is your first reaction to that statement? Is it negative or positive? When we hear the word problem, we automatically assume that it is bad or negative. But let's hear the rest of what the person was going to say. "I have inherited 10 million dollars! What am I going to do with all that money?" I think we could consider that a positive problem, couldn't we? Wouldn't we all like to have that kind of problem?

Now that we know the word "problem" is usually thought of as negative, why don't we change the word "problem" to a word that has no emotional content for us, one that is neither negative nor positive. We can change the word "problem" to the word <u>situation</u>. If someone came up to you and said, "I have a situation I need your help with?" how would you react emotionally? There is no emotional content in it for you. It is strictly a neutral word. From now on, we no longer have problems. We only have situations that need to be solved. (Since you are used to the word "problem", I will continue to use it throughout the book.)

Successful people are problem/situation solvers. In fact, most problem solvers usually come up with multiple ways to solve a particular problem. We, if we are lucky, can come up with one solution (and the majority of the time, it is not the correct solution). How do problem solvers manage to come up with the right solution?

First of all, they are positive thinkers. They believe in their abilities and have confidence in themselves. Have you ever noticed that there is always one person in the office or the classroom that is a problem solver? It seems as if everyone turns to them for answers and solutions because they are always right. Problem solving appears to come so easily for them.

Here is a hypothetical case:

> The boss calls everyone into his office. (This morning the office problem solver is out of the office on a business appointment). The boss lets everyone settle down. He states there is a big problem. He needs everyone to brainstorm to come up with a solution. The worst part of this is that we must have a solution in one hour. Everyone gets up out of their chairs, leaving his office. They <u>seem</u> to be calm, cool and collected.
>
> At this point, I wish someone had a video camera set up outside of his office door to record the looks on their faces. The difference in their faces, as they walked through his door, is almost beyond description. I think sheer panic would closely describe it as well as anything else.
>
> As time passes, the deadline gets closer. The atmosphere is so tense and stressful, you could literally "cut it with a knife". These people are running around like "chickens with their heads cut off". It is as if they were "bouncing off the walls and ceiling". Got the picture?
>
> Our problem solver has now returned to the office, calm, relaxed, and in control. The first thing he notices is the tension and stress. He walks over to the nearest person and asks, "What in the world has happened this morning? Did the President die or something?" The co-worker replied, "It is almost that bad."
>
> He proceeds to tell the problem solver the situation; then the co-worker looks down at his watch and almost screams, "And we only have thirty minutes left to come up with the answer!" As soon as the problem is explained to the problem solver, the problem solver asks, "Has anyone come up with...?" You can, at this point, see the co-worker mentally hit his forehead. There is a look of amazement on his face. He says to our problem solver, "I can't believe I didn't see the answer. It was right in front of my face. It is so simple!"

If it was so simple, why didn't all the people in the office come up with the solution? Solutions can be amazingly simple when you know how to stay relaxed and manage stressful people, and situations! (Has the above situation ever happened to you by any chance?)

Let's examine the co-worker's emotional, mental, and physical states. What were the adjectives I used to describe the co-worker's states?

Panicked, tense, stressed?

Are you able to think, much less solve problems, when you are in these states of mind, along with your physical body being tense? (and you are probably on the way to having a headache "this big"!)

What were the adjectives I used to describe our problem solver?

Calm, relaxed, in control

One of the main points in this book is to impress upon you the importance of staying relaxed, in other words keeping your "cool". Think about what happens when you get nervous.

Let's return to our problem solver. Would you say that he walked into a stressful situation with stressful people? Did he allow his co-workers to affect him? Of course not! If he had, he would never have been able to arrive at a solution. He stayed relaxed and in control, rather than tense and distressed. But how did he achieve staying relaxed, while managing the stress, and staying in control?

This is what we will be discussing in the next chapter: the importance of relaxation for staying relaxed, managing stress, and achieving control of self.

RELAXATION

What is relaxation? It comes from the root word "relax." The dictionary's definition is:

"to become looser or less firm, as the muscles; to become less tense or stern, as one's features; ...to become easier in manner...to rest from effort, application, or work."

Wow! There is a lot to think about here, isn't there? So, which one should we tackle first? Why don't we just take them in order? I believe we will!

To be able to think clearly, we must relax the body completely, "to become looser, or less firm; as the muscles; which includes...becoming less tense or stern, as ones features,...to become easier in manner...to rest from effort, application, or work." All of these have some relationship with the physical body.

I ask you again, how can you think clearly when your body is "tied up in knots"? Are you focusing on what you need to think about or the discomfort or pain in your body?

Recall the group of people in my problem-solving story. We will go into more details about why these people could not relax. What were the stressors in the story?

1. Boss calls everyone in unexpectedly.
2. States "We have a problem."
3. States emphatically, "We must have a solution."
4. The worst stressor of all, an unrealistic time limit.

What did the stressors' create?

1. FEAR - of the unknown
2. WORRY - about the problem
3. ANXIETY - uncertainty of the outcome
4. PANIC - when the thought process stops

All of these conditions were in progress, in one degree or another, with the people in the office. In walks our problem solver, calm, relaxed, and in control.

How did he manage to stay relaxed, calm, and in control? He learned, either through experience, by attending a stress management seminar, or more than likely through relaxation techniques, and perhaps he has also read books about relaxation.

There are many philosophies and disciplines on relaxation. Zen, Yoga, Tai-Chi, The Silva Method, Aikido, and Transcendental Meditation to name a few of them. These are all structured disciplines. You must have structure and follow a specific set of instructions, for the brain to form a new habit. All of these disciplines agree that deep breathing is an essential part in training the body for the process of relaxing.

Some of these disciplines start the relaxation process at the feet, going upward toward the head. Others start at the head and go downward toward the feet. I prefer the latter. Why? Well, which way does gravity pull on the body? Up or Down? I like to do THINGS the easy way. For me, starting at the feet (Watch out, Mr. Spock!) is illogical. By starting at the head, each muscle group relaxes and pushes downward on the others, which in turn helps the next group to relax until I have reached my feet. Do whatever makes you comfortable and relaxed. After you feel your body totally relaxed, it is the time to relax your mind.

I already know your next question. How do I relax my mind? The disciplines we discussed above have another factor in common. You relax the mind by focusing on a visualized place (a place where you have been some time in your past) where you were safe, relaxed, comfortable, and calm. The following is my choice:

> When I was a child, in back of our house were woods,
> wild flowers, a creek, small animals and so on. I loved walking
> there for the peace and oneness I felt with the woods. Sometimes
> I would climb a tree and just look up into the sky.

This is still the place that I visualize today. I re-experience the sensations I had then; sight, sound, touch, smell, thoughts, and feelings. This process helps my mind to relax.

Stop and think about your "relaxation place". Whenever you feel the need for relaxation, relax the body and the mind with the exercises previously discussed. You can do this anywhere - home, school, or work. No matter where you are, there is always a bathroom, isn't there? You must make the time. You are the most important person on this planet. If you do not take care of yourself, who will? Who knows your needs better than you?

When you set aside time on a daily basis to practice relaxation, you will discover several advantages. You will find you have the qualities of being:

1. Relaxed
2. Focused
3. Stress free
4. Emotionally stable
5. **IN CONTROL**

How are you in control? Instead of your thoughts racing 90 miles an hour, you are focusing and concentrating on what you need (which is relaxation) by <u>directing</u> and <u>controlling</u> your thoughts to a <u>specific place and time</u>. The same applies when you are using your "Goal Room" exercise. <u>You are</u> directing and controlling your thoughts for a specific purpose - **your goal.**

The most amazing discovery is the enjoyment of relaxing. It will become such a pleasurable experience that you will wonder why you didn't do it sooner! I cannot say it often enough. You must <u>make</u> the time on a daily basis if you want your dreams to come true. Your dreams are the goals you have set for yourself.

I want to hear from you. Write to me in care of the publisher about how you have made your dreams come true. I would really like to hear from you!

EXERCISE FOR RELAXATION

1. Close your eyes.
2. Take several deep breaths to relax the body. Visualize your "special place" to relax your mind.
3. Starting at either your head or feet, pretend, make believe, or imagine that particular part of your body relaxing.
4. Go to the next connecting part of your body, and so on, until your whole body is relaxed. If starting at the head, the next area would be the neck, shoulders, etc. If starting at the feet, the next area would be the ankles, calves, knees, etc.
5. Before you open your eyes, go to your "special place" (as described above). Re-experience your surroundings! When you are ready, proceed to number six.
6. Take several deep breaths; then open your eyes.

You should feel totally relaxed and at peace with yourself and your surroundings. It is a feeling that will definitely "grow on you".

MANAGING STRESS

What is the definition of stress? The dictionary states that stress is:

> *"to strain; pressure; especially, force exerted upon a body, that tends to strain or deform its shape-urgency; distress-to afflict greatly; to afflict with pain or anguish; to harass; to make miserable; unhappy, anxious, etc; to trouble."*

We have several ideas presented in this definition. To what are these ideas referring? **YOUR BODY**. How many of you feel as if you have wasted money on stress management seminars? Are you stress-free?

If you are not stress-free, then how do you go about becoming stress free? Think about my problem solver. He stayed calm, relaxed, and in control. We are stress-free when we stay calm, relaxed, and in control.

What is the opposite of distressed? Relaxation. Stress can not affect you when you stay relaxed. Practice handling stressful situations in your "Goal Room". Choose the situations that would normally affect you. Keep your <u>desired end result</u> in mind, so when that particular situation happens in the "real world", you can and will handle it in the correct or proper manner. When you are calm and relaxed, you are in control of the once stressful situation or person.

Here is an example of a stressful situation which I believe we can all relate to - our first oral book report.

> Oral book report, oh my God, does the teacher mean that I am going to HAVE to get up in front of the <u>whole</u> class and speak?

What was your first reaction? Absolute, total **FEAR**!!!

HOW CAN I GET UP IN FRONT OF THE CLASS AND
MAKE A FOOL OUT OF MYSELF?

The next item you become aware of is that writing is not the same as speaking (brother, do I understand that one).

Now you re-write your book report so it sounds as if you were talking. Next on the agenda is practicing in front of someone (probably a family member, who really helps the situation by making fun of you). In your mind, you are anticipating what is going to happen to you when you get in front of everyone.

What exactly were you thinking? I would bet money you thought about all the things that could go wrong. What actually happened? All the things you thought about happening went wrong!
What were the stressors?

1. Fear - public speaking
2. Anxiety - re-writing
3. Shame - ridicule/laughter from family and classmates
4. Guilt - if I don't do well...
5. Panic - your turn to speak
6. Exhaustion - after the report has been given

How could we have avoided all of the above? By having the positive support we needed. If we had that positive support from the day we were born, we would not have stressful situations as adults. Give yourself the positive support you need. Practice in your "Goal Room" with this exercise:

EXERCISE FOR RELIEVING STRESS

1. Close your eyes.
2. Take several deep breathes to relax the body. Visualize your special place to relax the mind.
3. Watch yourself in the first room, the "Situation Room" under a stressful situation. See how you reacted, what you said, how you felt, and what was said to you. Remember every detail.
4. Enter the second door into your "Rehearsal Room". Visualize yourself staying calm, relaxed, and in control. Feel yourself responding in the way you think is proper for this particular situation; acting, answering, and feeling correctly.
5. Enter the third door into your "Goal Room". You are there in reality, calm, relaxed, and in control. You are responding, acting, and feeling the situation NOW. Perform every detail you saw in your "Rehearsal Room".

By staying calm and relaxed, you are not "reacting" to others. Doesn't the word re-act mean:

"to repeat or revert to a previous condition"?

We do not want to repeat a mistake by reacting to stressful people or situations. We can learn and will take the proper, necessary action to resolve the situation.

In other words, we can come up with solutions when before our thought processes were blocked by stress. Stress seems to cascade, like dominoes, with a will of it's own. Thank goodness, relaxation works the same way.

This sounds wonderful, Patricia, but I still do not understand how **I control stress**! You control stress **by what you are thinking**. This is why you are practicing with your "Goal Room" exercises. You are learning to control your re-actions. You are learning to **ACT** instead of reverting to previous negative behaviors.

What have these previous negative behaviors achieved? Negative behaviors have put you in the situation you are now experiencing and only you know what these situations are. You also know how to correct them.

Here is another well known saying: "Practice makes perfect." (Well, as close to perfect as is humanly possible. After all, how many perfect people do you know?) Practice your "Goal Room" exercises until you become what you are practicing. (Remember you are an actor or actress.) Learn to recognize people in "DIStress". Learn to recognize "DIStressful situations". This is easily accomplished when you learn to stay relaxed and in control. You will find that you can no longer be pulled into stressful situations.

HEALTH

Before we continue with this chapter, do you remember in Chapter Two I asked you to think about someone you considered to be successful? At this point, does your successful person have all of the characteristics or qualities we have discussed? Are they self-confident? Do they have a good self-esteem? Do they think positively? Do they set goals? Are they problem solvers? Do they stay relaxed? Do they know how to manage stress? Most assuredly they do possess these qualities. How do all these qualities relate to health?

Before I answer the last question, the following is another story I would like you to consider.

There is always one person in the office/school who seems to never get sick. The flu or colds can go around the office three times in one season, but they just stay healthy. Out of curiosity one day, I walked up to the healthy person I knew, and I asked, "Don't you ever get sick?" Can you guess what their reply was?

"No, I never get sick; **I AM always healthy.**"

What are the two most important words in your vocabulary? I AM. These two words state a belief about yourself. The person believed they were always healthy, so what was the result? They were always healthy. Sure, every once in a while they may get sick, but look at their recovery time. They may be down two or three days, while each of us would probably be sick for weeks instead of days. The occurrence of their illnesses might only be every four or five years, if that often.

How often do you get sick? How often do you have sinus problems, hay fever problems, allergy problems, high blood pressure problems, stomach problems, headaches, the flu, or whatever afflicts you? If you have health problems of any kind, what has caused them?

YOU HAVE CAUSED THEM.

You have caused them by the negativity you have attracted into your life. How have you attracted negativity into your life? By your thoughts.

Do you want to change and be a healthy person? Then change the way you are thinking. How long did it take for you to have bad health? How many years of stress, worry, anger, blame, shame, and guilt, etc., has caused this situation? (Remember the majority of us were not born with these afflictions.) **Number one** on everyone's goal list (no matter your age) should be, "I am in perfect health."

We have to re-train the body to be in perfect health by forming a new habit. The new habit is "I am in perfect health." Do you want perfect health tomorrow, next week, five years from now, or do you want it now? We can live only in the present. What we do now determines what we will have tomorrow, next week, or five years from now.

Would you like to know the most negative programmer in the world? The "boob tube", otherwise known as the television. What do advertisers program you for every winter?

"The cold and flu season is coming on. Be sure to have plenty of
_____ in the house>"

When spring comes around, what do they say?

"It is the hay fever, allergy, sinus season. Be sure to have _____
in the house." "You have a headache 'this big' -get_____."
"You have an upset stomach - you need _____." "You can't take
aspirin - get_____."

Please, do not misunderstand me. If you have a health problem, see your doctor. If you have broken your arm, no amount of positive thinking after the fact is going to change your broken arm.

After you have seen your doctor, no matter the reason, he sends you home and tells you to do what? Rest.

What is relaxation? It is resting the body and the mind. By resting the body and the mind, this allows your immune system to strengthen. When your immune system strengthens, you become healthier.

What I am saying is, why not avoid health problems by changing the way you think and how you ACT? Doctors, magazines, books, and seminars all say that stress affects your health.

So why are you unhealthy? Because you never knew how or why you were unhealthy. Do you have the skills in your power right now, to change the state of your health?

When you are healthy, you can focus on those things that you want in life, giving those things the positive energy they need instead of giving the problem (your illness) the negative energy which allows it to continue.

44

When you are sick, what are you thinking about?

1. "God, do I feel bad."
2. "I am so achy."
3. "I have a fever, and it still hasn't gone down yet."
4. "If I have to blow my nose one more time..."
5. "I feel like I would have to die before I get better."

Is this what you prefer to think about, your illness? Reenforcing what is wrong? Do you really want to die? Or would you prefer to be healthy by directing your energy to your goals that will help you to attain perfect health?

I am assuming (you know what happens when you assume) that all of you are exercising, getting plenty of rest, and eating nutritionally. In all things, we must (need to) learn moderation. Overeating, anorexia, and bulimia are three of America's biggest health concerns. Are these caused from moderation in our thinking, or are they caused from going to extremes in our thinking?

What are some of the causes of these problems? A poor self-esteem and a lack of self-confidence seem to be the most common factors, and a total feeling of a lack of control in ones' life. I know from personal experience. At one point in my life I weighed 240 pounds. In my case, my overeating stemmed from my childhood experiences, which created a lack of self-esteem, self-confidence, and the feeling of being out of control.

I realized, when I was in the process of changing my life, WHY weight loss programs and dieting never worked for me. I wasn't losing weight for me but because others were always "on my case" about my weight. All I could hear was "You are fat because you cannot control your eating habits."

When I started to change the person I was into the person I wanted to be, and then became that person inside, I decided it was time to change the outside also. I did it for me. It was my choice. I had to understand that food represented unconditional love to me because of my low self-esteem. Now that I could give love to myself, I no longer needed the comfort of food to do it for me.

I worked for nine years building the qualities of a successful person, all of which depended on having a good self-esteem and self-confidence. I knew I was overweight, and I did not need people to constantly remind me of my weight problem. I lived with that fact 24 hours a day. Until I could love myself, I was unable to change my eating habits. When I made the choice to lose the weight because I wanted to, I dropped one hundred pounds. It came off so easily; I was amazed.

Before, every time I had gone on a diet, it was an absolute struggle to stay on the diet. To add insult to injury, I always added pounds after every diet! It seemed as if I always "found" the weight that others had "lost"!

Why was it easy this time? Because all the reasons for being and staying fat were gone due to the rise in my confidence and self-esteem. When the weight came off, my health improved. I will also admit that during the weight loss process the positive feedback I received from others felt wonderful. What did the positive feedback do for my self-esteem? My self-esteem went through the ceiling, of course!

By practicing and imagining my desired end result, my whole life changed. It does not have to take years for you. You can change your life now.

This is the exercise for health problems:

EXERCISE FOR HEALTH

1. Close your eyes.
2. Take several deep breaths to relax the body. Visualize your "Special place" to relax the mind.
3. See yourself in the first room as you are now with your health problem.
4. Open the door and go into the "Rehearsal Room".
5. Visualize yourself in perfect health, doing the things you were not able to do due to your health problem.
6. Imagine what it would feel like to be healthy.
7. Open the door into your "Goal Room".
8. You are now in your "Goal Room", experiencing your perfect health, feeling your body responding perfectly. Doing the things you were unable to do because of your poor health.

Whenever I have heard the word "healthy", there is another word that usually accompanies it. Do you have an idea what that word might be? (No, it is not wealthy or wise!) I will give you a clue. It starts with the same letter as healthy.

Have you guessed it yet? It is HAPPY! How often have you heard, "She is a happy, healthy person"? I have heard that expression all my life. Have YOU ever HEARD of an unhappy, healthy person? No, of course not.

I will explain what I mean by happy. Happy can have several definitions. The following is my favorite:

> *"...having, showing, or causing a feeling of great pleasure, joy, contentment, etc.; joyous; glad; pleased; satisfied."*

Hopefully you know or have known someone like this in your life. I have known very few people in my life, that were truly a pleasure to be around. But I found that when I was around those few people who were happy, I could be in the depths of depression (commonly known as "the pits", thank you Erma Bombeck), and this particular person would raise my spirits without any conscious effort on my part. He or she was a genuinely happy person. They were not only happy with themselves but with all aspects of their life and everything going on around them. When I walked away from them, it seemed as if some of my burdens had been lifted from my shoulders.

As luck would have it, I am fortunate enough to have two such people in my family: my aunt and sister-in-law. They both happen to share the same name, Nancy. These two people brought sunshine into my life as a child. I knew there was a kind word or hug whenever they were around. All they expected from me was to be me. Through all the changes I have made in my life, they have maintained this consistency of unconditional love. They have been a joyous experience in my life, and I thank them now for wanting to be a part of my life. I have always thought of them as truly happy and loving people. Their smiles lit up my entire being.

Is your successful person a happy, healthy person? Is this person the kind of person you would like to be around, especially if you are in "the pits"? Would you like to be a happy, healthy person? Would you like to know that others like to be around you because of the inner happiness you radiate?

You know the procedure. Go to your "Goal Room" and practice the exercises which make you feel good about yourself. When you feel good about yourself, others will feel this positive energy radiating from you. Before you know it, you will be a happy, healthy person also.

LAUGHTER IS <u>YOUR</u> BEST MEDICINE.

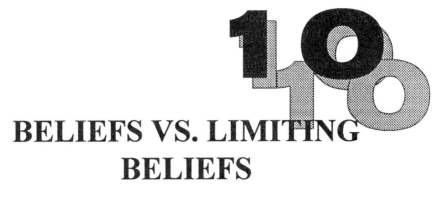

BELIEFS VS. LIMITING
BELIEFS

Shall we take a ride to the dictionary again to discover what the definition of "belief" is? Webster's says it is:

"an acceptance of something as true; anything believed; an opinion; expectation; judgement."

How old were you when you started believing in "something as true"?

Almost from birth, you started "believing, trusting, and accepting things as true." As a baby, we accept the love and care of our caregivers. We did not question what we received, whether it was unconditional love or total abandonment. As children, we accepted how we were treated as "normal". Why did we not question this?

Scientists have discovered that until the age of six or seven, children think inductively. What does that mean? It means that we are not able to deduce (figure out with our thought processes) the validity of information we are receiving. We store the information until we reach the age of six or seven. Our thinking process then changes to deductive thinking. Deductive thinking means we are able to understand using stored information what is being said to us, and to understand what is going on around us. Under the age of six or seven, we are not able to second guess whatever is being said to us. That is why children are literal.

I believe the following is a good example of inductive, literal thinking:

Remember as a child when you wanted to go outside to play. Your mother came into your room and said, "You must pick up all your toys from the floor before going outside to play", and she left your room. You proceeded to pick up the toys, placing them everywhere, on the bed, on the shelves, and on the dresser. In the meantime, your mother came back to check to see if you had picked up your toys. She saw how you had put your toys "up". She was angry. She went to the door and called you inside. She said,

"I thought I told you to pick up your toys before you went outside to play." You reply, "I did, Mommie." The child is totally confused as to the cause of her anger.

What is missing from this story? Did the child do what she was told to do? Remembering that children, until the age of six or seven, think inductively and literally, let us examine the situation.

What, literally, did Mother say?
1. To pick up all of the toys from the floor.
   What did the child do?
2. Literally picked up the toys from the floor, placing them around the room on various objects.
   Why did Mother get angry when seeing where the toys were placed?
3. She meant for them to be placed in the toy box.
   Why is the child now confused over Mothers' reaction?
4. She is unable, due to age, to second guess what Mother really wanted her to do.

The child is not at the age where her thinking processes have changed from inductive to deductive thinking. She has not yet learned, through repetition, exactly what her Mother wanted from her. She literally did what Mother said.

What does this have to do with belief? As children, we are asked and told to do many things that are for our protection, such as not to touch hot burners and not to run out into the street. We learn to obey our parents at an early age because we do not have the skill to question why, much less the skill to understand the answer. We trust and believe in our caregivers. We learn to accept what is told to us "as true".

Here is another story I would like to share with you. I heard this story several years ago. The story has a name. It is called the "Famous Family Roast Beef" story. I think it is an excellent example of how we acquire our beliefs.

This is a story about two newlyweds. Their names are Mary and John. Mary really loved John and John thought Mary was the most wonderful girl in the world. They had been married only three months when Mary decided she would do something very special for John. She decided she would make the famous family roast beef. This was made only on very special occasions. She took her week's allowance and went to the store. There she spent almost all of it on the roast beef. (As you all know, when couples first get married, the majority of them are on a very strict budget.) She came home from the market. She thought that she would make this the most perfect meal she had ever served. She decided to use her wedding china, candlelabras, and silverware that they had received at their wedding shower. Because John loved Mary so much, he decided to take off early from work so that he could come home and help Mary with the preparations. When he arrived home, he found her in the kitchen preparing the famous family roast beef. She was salting and peppering it and seasoning it just right. Then, just before she put it into the pan, she picks up a butcher knife and cuts off one inch from one end, then cuts off another inch from the other end. She picks up the roast beef, puts it into a pan, and puts the pan into the oven. John is very confused by what Mary has just done with the roast and says, "Hey, what are you doing? That is a whole week's food budget. We can't afford to throw any of it away." Mary turns around and says "What do you mean, what am I doing?" John replied, "You just took a knife and cut one inch off one end and then cut another inch off the other end before you put it in the pan." Mary replies, "I don't know what you are talking about; that is just the way you make the famous family roast beef." Well, John didn't want to spoil the romantic evening, but he began to wonder about his wife. After the dinner was over though, he had to admit, it was the best roast beef he had ever eaten. He wondered if maybe there might be something to cutting the roast beef off on both ends. A couple of months later, Mary's mother called. She said, "You know John, you and Mary have not been over to dinner since you have been married. I would like for you to come over Sunday. I am making the famous family roast beef." John said, "Wonderful, we will be there." John and Mary arrived early so John could watch Mary's mother prepare the roast beef. He walked into the kitchen, and there she was, salting and peppering and seasoning the roast beef just right. Before she placed it in the pan, she picked up a knife and cut one inch from one end and another inch from the other end. She put it in the pan and placed the roast in the oven. John said, "Why do you do that?" Mary's mother replied, "Do what?" "Why do you cut one inch from one end and one inch from the other end before you put it in the pan?" The mother-in-law replied, "Well I don't know what you are talking about; this is just the way you make the famous family roast beef!" Again, John had to admit, he had never tasted anything better. John began to wonder if he were crazy, or if he had married into a crazy family! A few months after this, Mary's grandmother called. She said, "You know John, you and Mary have not been to my house for dinner, and if you will come I will make your favorite dish. Anything you want." Can you imagine what John asked for? The famous family roast beef! John said, "Well Grandma, can I come early and watch you make it?" She said she would love to have him come early, being very flattered that John would like to watch her cook. Well, John was so excited, he couldn't sleep. He got up early the next morning to go to Grandma's house. When he arrived, there was Grandma in the kitchen preparing the roast beef. She salts and peppers it and seasons it just right. She picks up the roast, puts it the pan, and puts it into the oven. And John says, "Hey, wait a minute, didn't you forget something?" Grandma says, "No, I don't think so. What could I have forgotten?" John says, "Well you didn't get a knife and cut one inch from one end and another inch from the other end." Grandma says, "Why in the world would I want to do that?" "Well that is how your daughter makes it, and that is the way your granddaughter makes it," replied John. Grandma stopped and thought for a moment and said, "Are they still doing that? Why I stopped doing that years ago...when I got a bigger pan!!!"

When we grow older, a habit has been formed, which is to accept, with no reservations, what the authority figures in our lives have told or shown us. These are the beliefs we live by all our lives.

In the above story, I hope we had a good laugh, but perhaps you need to examine your beliefs more closely. Why do I do the things I do? Why do I make the decisions I make? Upon what do I base these decisions? Are my beliefs helping me or hurting me?

Perhaps the following statements were said to you or about you that may have affected your beliefs about yourself?

1. "Why can't you be more like your brother/sister?"
2. "You will never amount to anything."
3. "You are going to be fat all your life if you keep eating like that."
4. "If your are born poor, you will always be poor."
5. "You have on so much make-up, you look like a _____."
6. "Can't you do anything right?"
7. "Why can't you make good grades like _____?"
8. "You are a born loser."
9. "You are so clumsy!"
10. "Don't do as I do, do as I say do!"

When these statements were said to you, how old were you? What did you think? How did you feel? Did you believe them? How many times were they said to you?

What has happened in these instances is that the statements have become a part of your belief system. They will be with you the rest of your life in some degree or another unless you decide to change them.

How have they affected your self-esteem and self-confidence? The decisions you make in your life are based on the beliefs instilled in you as a child.

Here is another example of how a belief can affect you in your adult life. I will choose one of the above as the example.

> A two year old is learning how to drink from a glass and drops it. The caregiver screams at the child, "You are so clumsy, can't you hold onto your glass?" The child is three and reaches for a cookie and drops it on the floor. The caregiver yells, "Can't you pay attention to what you are doing? You are always so clumsy. You drop everything you touch."

This continues throughout the child's life and into adulthood. This phrase has been repeated so many times, over and over again, that clumsiness has become a habit. The adult thinks, "If I pick this up, will I drop it?" As a result of that thought, remembering that we think in mental images, the adult drops everything he touches without realizing **why** dropping things always happens to him.

The sad part of this story is that our caregivers did not know the damage they were creating. I believe, with all my heart, that our caregivers never wanted to knowingly hurt us, their child; yet, look at the results.

Why are our caregivers the way they are? They were teaching us the way they had been taught. From whom did they learn it? They learned from their parents, our grandparents. From whom did our grandparents learn it, etc.?

I am not offering an excuse for the way in which you were raised. What I am saying is your caregivers were doing the best they knew how, by using the tools available to them from their childhoods. These tools are not the tools we have available today.

If you have children, what negative beliefs have you passed along to them? Is this the kind of inheritance you want to leave them? If you are planning to have children, what kind of tools do you want them to have to improve their lives?

You cannot change the past, so why do you live in it and blame others for your shortcomings, no matter what their origins? You have the power to change what you are into what you want to be, but you must move out of the past and into the present.

THROW AWAY your old beliefs, the ones that are keeping you from achieving success. Get out of the "guilt, blaming, shaming, fault finding game". Examine, in depth, your beliefs and what has caused you to be the way you are today. You don't want your children to have the same problems, you do?

For our next exercise, I will choose the example of being clumsy. Use your "Goal Room" exercise as follows:

EXERCISE FOR CHANGING A LIMITING BELIEF

1. Close your eyes.
2. Take several deep breaths to relax the body. Visualize your "Special place" to relax the mind.
3. Visualize the "Situation Room".
4. Re-play an incident when you were clumsy. What were you thinking before the clumsy act; how were you feeling, what did you say (if anything), and what were the circumstances surrounding the act. Remember every detail.
5. Enter the "Rehearsal Room" and see yourself handling the situation with total confidence, imagining how good you feel, responding correctly in every detail.
6. Enter your "Goal Room" actually re-living the experiences of all the details you created in the second room.

If clumsiness is one of your beliefs that needs to be changed, how many years has your clumsiness been a habit? How many days does it take to form a new habit? Before you do anything that you might normally be clumsy doing, **STOP** a moment and visualize yourself doing it right. **Expect your visualization to happen correctly, and it will**. It will happen exactly as you imagine it.

The ten examples I gave previously are limiting beliefs. Perhaps none or some limiting beliefs are in your past. You have been limited in what you believe you can do. Do you choose to stay limited, or do you choose to be the person you would like to be? Are you going to take the time, energy, effort and practice it requires to make the changes you want in your life?

It is up to you.

POSITIVE
IMAGING/SPEAKING

We will break this chapter down into two parts, positive imaging/thinking and positive speaking. First remember, as human beings, we think in mental images. Since we do not communicate with mental images to others, we must communicate with words.

Concerning our exercises in our second room, we visualize our desired end result. When you want to communicate with someone, do you project thoughts to them or do you use words? And... what are the words you choose to describe your mental image when you speak? Are the words negative or positive? Are you "saying what you mean and meaning what you say?" Below are some examples:

1. Don't slam the door.
2. Don't forget your _____.
3. I can't believe_____.

We will look at these one by one and examine them to see if we are saying what we mean or meaning what we say. (Remembering that we **THINK** in mental images.)

1. What is your mental image when you say, "Don't slam the door"?

You should already know the answer. Your mental image is of a door slamming; yet that is not what you wanted.

What did you want? You wanted the door to be closed quietly, softly, or gently. But you did not **say** that.

2. What is your mental image when you say, "Don't forget your..."?

Your mental image is of leaving something behind.

What did you want? To remember to bring_____ with you. Did you forget, or did you remember?

> 3. What is your mental image when you say,
> "I can't believe..."?

Your mental image is <u>not to believe</u> what someone is telling you. What did you mean to say? "This is amazing... this is surprising...I would have never imagined that this could happen!"

Do you have communication problems? Are you always able to "get across" what you are saying to others? If not, you are probably saying what you <u>do not</u> want instead of saying what it is you <u>do</u> want.

Every time you open your mouth to speak, you become a verbal artist. What kind of a verbal artist are you? I would like for you to consider this thought. Have you noticed how America's language has become a conglomeration of exaggerations and slang phrases? We use these phrases because we want to **stress** our point.

This next story illustrates how we believe we are saying what we mean, but the opposite is true.

> Return to your past, when you were four or five years old. You were playing in the house. You looked out the window and saw your friends playing together. You were no longer happy playing by yourself in the house, so you went and asked your mother if you could go outside with your friends. For some reason, your mother said no. You did not understand why you couldn't go outside, but you do know from experience, if you made more noise, you might get to go outside. Sure enough, your mother came in and said, "You are too loud, and you are giving me a headache. Go outside and play". All right! This was what you wanted! Before your mother could change her mind, (which we know parents can do in a moment for no reason at all!), you literally started running to the door. As you were about to reach the door, do you remember what your mother hollered? **DON'T SLAM THE DOOR!** And what did you promptly do? <u>You slammed the door!</u>

Why did you slam the door? Because the mental picture in your mind was one of a slamming door. Your mother shouldn't have been mad when you slammed the door. You did exactly what she told you to do.

Now wait a minute, Patricia; she said, "Don't slam the door." That is correct. What was your mental image? What did mother really want you to do? She wanted you to close the door quietly, softly, or gently. But is that what she said? Did she say what she meant? No.

56

Here is an example of how the mental image is changed in the child's mind.

When the child got up and started running towards the door, the mother said, "Patricia, close the <u>door quietly, softly or gently.</u>" The child slowed down when she got to the door, very carefully she reached for the door handle and slowly turned the door knob. Almost on tip toes, she goes through the door, holding the door so that it would close quietly behind her.

What is the difference in the mental image of "slamming the door" and "closing the door quietly"? Which mental image is what "we don't want", and which mental image is what "we do want"? Which is the negative mental image and which is the positive mental image?

Every time you open your mouth to speak, you are a verbal artist, painting your mental image/picture. The sole purpose of words is to communicate your mental image into someone else's mind in the form of a mental picture. Instead of a paintbrush in your hand, you are using words to paint a picture of what you are thinking.

I will ask you again. When you communicate with others, do you always paint a clear picture of what is in your mind? Do you choose the right words to describe exactly what it is you want? If you have communication problems of any kind, I suggest you re-read this chapter again, and then practice in your "Goal Room". Learn to say "exactly what you mean and mean what you say". Learn to speak in such a manner, so that whoever hears you will have no doubts about what you are saying or meaning!

SUMMARY

We have discussed and reviewed the ten qualities of becoming a successful human being. Do we agree that each quality has its own definition, but that to realize ones' fullest potential, one must have a high self-confidence and a high self-esteem level? Each quality has its own function. One quality does not do the job of the other quality. But to be successful, we must use all of the ten qualities, which are based on self-esteem and self-confidence.

I suggest, through my own experience, that you begin with self-confidence or self-esteem. Afterwards, you may choose any quality, numbers 3-10, in any order that is comfortable for you. You may have other qualities you would like to add to my list. Do whatever feels right for you!

A reminder - when you are practicing to achieve your desired end result, to which room, 1, 2, or 3, will you give all of your energy? The third room, which is your "Goal Room". This is the room in which you experience your desired end result. After you have made your change, this is the procedure you will follow:

FOLLOW-UP EXERCISE

1. Close your eyes.
2. Take several deep breaths to relax the body and mind.
3. Visualize your SECOND room. Use this room as a reminder of what you will be giving all of your energy to in your "Goal Room".
4. Visualize yourself, as if you are watching a movie. See your change as you want it to be. Take as much time as you need to hear, speak, or feel. Enter your "Goal Room".
5. Once in your "Goal Room", you are experiencing everything you have seen yourself rehearse in the second room. Remember, you are now an actor or actress playing your part, creating your life the way you want it to be.
6. Open your eyes.

You can repeat this exercise as often as your schedule allows. I practice four to five times a day or more. The more you practice with this exercise, the faster you will become comfortable with your changes and the faster you will see your desired end results. This book is for you (which I hope will be a pleasurable and exciting experience).

In every chapter, I have emphasized practicing. Why? Without practice, whatever you want will never become a "part of you". You will slip back into the "old habits". Those habits are very comfortable and require no time or conscious effort on your part. You will then question yourself and probably wonder if all the time you are spending is really worth it to make your changes. Only you can answer that question. How badly do you want to change? Do you have a burning desire to change?

Patricia, what are habits that I use everyday without conscious effort? The following are examples of ordinary, everyday habits that you perform without conscious effort:

> Is anyone reading this book of driving age? Were you born with the knowledge of how to drive a car? No? Then what did you have to do to learn to drive a car? Any musicians reading this book? Secretaries? CPA's? Football players? Cheerleaders? Teachers? Actors? Editors? Lawyers? Doctors?

No matter what you have chosen to do in life, you had to practice. It took time, energy, effort, and practice on your part to become who you are today. The same is true when you are changing into who you want to become. The new changes will take time, energy, effort, and practice just as the old habits did when you first learned them!

NOW, LET'S TALK ABOUT MAKING MONEY! (At last! I bet you thought I would never get around to it!) If you had, and used, all of the above qualities, do you think you would have any problems making money? Believe it or not, money is the easiest of all things in the world to acquire.

We Americans are very lucky that we can get employment anywhere or in any profession we wish. If we need extra money, we are allowed to get another job. Yes, I mean allowed.

Look at other countries, where people are told how much education they can expect and what kind of job they will receive upon graduation. They are not allowed to have extra jobs or to earn extra money. In some countries, the majority of their people are unemployed and starving. This condition is happening all over the world.

Yes, we may have a six or seven percent unemployment problem in our nation, and we have the homeless, but there are jobs available. Are you "too good" or "better than" anyone else to accept a job that is not exactly what you want? Would you rather be supported by our government (which is really you and me from the tax money we pay each year when we are working)? How does living on welfare raise you self-confidence or self-esteem?

I have worked in jobs that I did not particularly like or where the money was less than what I would normally earn, but I have always been employed. Maybe I was not doing the job I wanted to do, but I stayed with the job until I found another that

60

<u>was</u> what I wanted and paid better. Use your "Goal Room" exercise to visualize yourself making the money you deserve!

I am not saying this world is fair, or just. What I am saying is that I continue to find what I want in my life by using my "Goal Room" exercises and not by depending on the world to be "just or fair". I keep putting out that positive energy to attract to me what **I** want to have in life. At the writing of this book, I have three jobs, all of which I love. (I have four jobs if you include writing this book!)

Wouldn't working at a job you love, making the kind of money you deserve, and being around people you enjoy be something you would like to have? Then use your "Goal Room" exercise to imagine yourself in this kind of job situation.

I realized years ago that I did not <u>have</u> to do anything in this world I was not happy doing. I <u>choose</u> the people I want to be with. I <u>choose</u> the people I want to be my friends. I work at the kind of job I <u>choose</u>. I have **choice**.

YOU have <u>choice</u>. Now is the time for you to decide! <u>Choose</u> what the rest of your life will be. (Guard your thoughts, thinking only of positive and constructive ideas to help you achieve your desired end results.)

The responsibility for your life is now in <u>YOUR HANDS</u>!

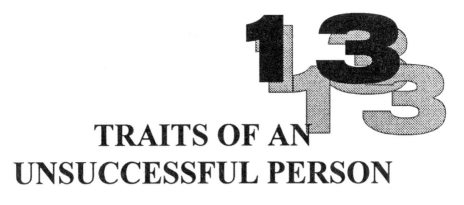

TRAITS OF AN UNSUCCESSFUL PERSON

What are the traits of an unsuccessful person? Obviously the opposite of the qualities of a successful person. I have chosen the following traits because they seem to be common to the majority of us.

1. Negative Thinking
2. Procrastination
3. Unhappy/Unhealthy
4. Fear
5. Anger
6. Denial
7. What If / If Only
8. I Can't Syndrome

In the following chapters we will cover the traits of an unsuccessful person.

If you have noticed, I have not used the word fail or failure. I believe that is one word that should be removed from the English language or any other language for that matter.

Remember the story of Thomas Edison and his reply to others who said he was a failure? His reply was, "No, I am not a failure. I am only a failure if I repeat one of the experiments that I know does not work." We have been so conditioned to failure that we no longer are able to think in a positive manner. The following chapters will discuss our negative behaviors.

NEGATIVE THINKING

Before we discuss negative thinking, we need to know the definition of negative. The dictionary's definition of negative is:

1. *"to refuse; reject; veto"*
2. *"to deny; contradict"*
3. *"to prove false; disapprove"*
4. *"to counteract; neutralize"*

The dictionary's definition of negativity is:

"THE QUALITY OR CONDITION OF BEING NEGATIVE."

Apply the definition of negativity to your thinking. Most negative-thinking people have learned to think that way from childhood. They learned to "accept as true" the limiting beliefs placed upon them as children. Let us review previous examples:

1. "You are so stupid."
2. "You are clumsy."
3. "You are a born loser."

What a burden to live with these negative statements all of one's life. To these examples we add other negative beliefs, and our life truly does go from "bad to worse". It is like building a house. We keep adding negative thinking upon negative thinking until we have built a house in which we feel there is no escape. We continue adding doorless, windowless rooms until we have a mansion in which we wander aimlessly, never finding the way OUT! We attract people and situations into our life in the same manner. The following is an example of adding negativity in one's life. READY? SET, GO!

In an office there always seems to be one extremely negative person. (Ladies, forgive me. In my experience it is usually a woman.) If she isn't complaining about her children, it is her husband. If it isn't her husband, it is her in-laws (or out-laws, whichever the case may be). If it isn't her in-laws, it is her job. If it isn't her job, it is her supervisor/manager. If it isn't her supervisor/manager, it is her salary. If it isn't her salary, it is her health: her headache, stomachache, the flu that has lasted for 3 weeks, her sinuses, and allergies. (Don't misunderstand me Ladies. The men complain also.)

Some people have learned to use illness as a way to receive sympathy and attention for the love they feel is lacking in their life. What we receive instead is more negative energy, re-enforcing that it is "all right" to be ill to get that extra love and attention. This is called negative reinforcement.

A negative person complains about all the negativity in their life but does nothing positive to change his/her situation. Some people will create more negativity in order to receive the attention they think they deserve. (Ever hear someone say, "If something isn't going wrong in his/her life, he/she will create it.)

This is the kind of person that when you see them get up and walk towards your desk, you want to get up and run as fast as you possibly can in the other direction. All you can think about is, "Not today, please, not today. I do not want to listen to his/her endless problems today!" If you are able to get away from your desk, have you ever noticed that they follow you until they have you cornered? You are not even safe in the restroom!

I am talking from experience. When I was placing blame, who do you think I blamed for all the bad things in my life? Do you think I blamed myself? Who did I point my finger at? When I was pointing the finger out at the world, how many fingers were pointing back at me? Three. How can you blame others for who, what, and where you have chosen to be? No one is to blame for your negative thinking except you.

Yes, your parents, teachers, preachers, friends and you have contributed to the way you are, but you are in control of your destiny now. **You** are the person who was making the decisions that led you in the direction you now find yourself. You now have the tools to alter your direction, to make of your life what you choose.

When you realize that your "pity party" is getting you nowhere except causing you to lose more of your self-esteem and self-confidence, perhaps you will take control of your life. I had to reach the bottom (which is where you might possibly be at this moment). When I reached the bottom, I had nowhere else to go but UP! And boy, is the air great up here! Come up and join me by changing your life the way you want it to be!

EXERCISE FOR NEGATIVE THINKING

1. Close your eyes.
2. Take several deep breathes to relax the body.

3. Go to your "Special Place" to relax your mind.
4. Visualize yourself in the "Situation Room" when you were negative. Remember the details.
5. Enter into your "Rehearsal Room". Watch yourself being negative and changing that negativity (whether that negativity was a thought, word, or deed) to a positive end result.
6. Enter your "Goal Room". You are experiencing that positive person you have always wanted to be.
7. Open your eyes.

Believe me, it takes the same amount of energy to be positive as it takes to be negative. Think back to an experience when you were negative. What was your energy level? What was your energy level when you were positive? Of the two, which energy makes you feel the best?

I think you will discover you have more energy at the end of the day when you keep a positive attitude. You will also feel better about yourself, and the nicest part of all will be that others will notice the difference in you.

PROCRASTINATION

By now you should know the routine at the beginning of each chapter, which is another trip to the dictionary for the definition of the word "procrastinate". The definition is to:

"postpone, defer, delay, put off."

The dictionary's definition of "procrastination" is:

"The act or <u>habit</u> of procrastinating"

The dictionary's definition of "procrastinating is:

"To put off doing something until a future time; to postpone or defer taking action."

Procrastination is a habit, huh? I wonder why I would list procrastination as a negative trait of an unsuccessful person? Take a moment to consider an answer. What answer did you come up with?

I think I will tell you another story while you are thinking about the above question (sneaky, aren't I). Ladies, has this ever happened to YOU?

When I was growing up, my mother taught me to choose the night before what I wanted to wear the next day. I was raised to make sure everything I wore matched, i.e. shoes, underwear, purse, jewelry, etc.. To this day, I still pick out what I am going to wear the night before (except some days it doesn't seem to work out that way). On some mornings when I wake up, I will look at what I have chosen the night before and wonder what I was thinking of when I chose the outfit.

At this point, let me explain that **I am not** a morning person. I would like to shoot the person that said morning begins at dawn. I believe it should start at twelve noon. Because I am not a morning person, I literally run on automatic until ten-thirty in the morning. All of a sudden, it is like I have just opened my eyes and realized that I am at work. (Hello. Earth to Patricia!) Are any of you like this? As I said before, since I am on automatic, my mornings are planned down to the split second so I can sleep as long as possible. I do not have the time, nor the sense, to choose something else to wear.

Wondering where my taste for clothes went to last night, guess what I have to do? Yep, go to the closet and pick something else to wear. (Is my Texas accent showing?) I start at the beginning of the closet and work my way to the back. When I get to the end of the closet, what do I have to do? You got it! I start all over again. (I guess I thought something new was going to pop into my closet when I wasn't looking. You know how sneaky clothes get be!) By the time I have made my decision on what I will wear, I am twenty minutes late in my morning routine. Since my mornings are planned to the split second, what does this do to my day? I am always twenty minutes behind. I never seem to catch up.

Do you ever regain the time you have lost, whether through procrastination or any other source?

Okay guys, you didn't think I was going to leave you out, did you? This is a story for you. Of course, this story only applies to those of you men that have ever had a father, male caregiver, or have been married. Did I cover every male?

For the sake of simplicity I will use as a example a "father" in the story.

Your father comes home from work one evening and your mother says, "Honey, when are you going to clean out the car?" Your father replies, "I will clean the car this weekend." Saturday morning arrives, and your mother wakes up your father. He says, "Honey, let me sleep in this morning. I have worked hard all week and have looked forward to sleeping in." When your Dad awakens, he heads for the kitchen where your mother prepares his breakfast. He has the Saturday paper and reads it while your mother is making breakfast and continues reading it during breakfast. When breakfast is over, it is twelve o'clock.

Ladies, what comes on TV starting at twelve on Saturdays? A football game. (Guys, don't get me wrong, I love football!) When this one is over, Ladies, what comes on TV at three o'clock? Another football game! Ladies, what comes on the TV at six o'clock? Now tell me, what man in his right mind is going to clean out a car at nine o'clock in the dark?

Your mother asks your Dad, "But Honey, you said you would clean up the car." "I will - tomorrow," he replies. Sunday morning arrives, and your mother awakens your Dad and he says, "Honey, let me sleep just a little longer. I have to get up and go to work tomorrow." So, your mother leaves him to wake up on his own. Later, your Dad gets up and goes into the kitchen where your Mother again prepares breakfast. (Ladies, how big is the Sunday paper, and what is on TV at twelve, three, and six o'clock?) Your mother again says, "But Honey, you said you would clean up the car this weekend." Your father replies, "Don't worry about it, I will clean out the car when I get home tomorrow night."

Ladies, again, what man in his right mind is going to clean out the car on Monday evening? And what comes on the TV at eight o'clock? Monday night football!

Did you get a good laugh or chuckle out of the two stories? Did you recognize yourself in either story?

CAREFUL, here comes another nosy question. While you were NOT doing whatever you had been procrastinating about, what did you find yourself thinking about? Was there any pleasure in putting off what you were supposed to be doing, or were you thinking about why you really should be doing it?

Procrastination causes four of the most negative emotions we can create as a human being. These emotions are:

1. GUILT
2. BLAME
3. SHAME
4. ANGER

Whenever you procrastinate, you experience all of these emotions to some degree. Let us examine them.

1. GUILT--I really ought to do this.
2. BLAME--I am so lazy.
3. SHAME--Mother taught me better.
4. ANGER--Caused from the above.

Is it really worth putting yourself through these negative emotions? Do the above emotions build your self-esteem or lower your self-esteem? Do you like having a low self-esteem? How much pleasure do you derive when you are procrastinating?

Then WHY do you procrastinate? Because you learned to procrastinate from others! We make jokes about procrastination. But the jokes are not so funny, now that you realize what YOU have been doing to yourself.

71

To continue, when you are procrastinating, what are you saying to yourself in your mind? You say things to yourself that you would never allow anyone else to ever say! For instance:

"If I had only gone ahead and done_____ and not been so lazy, I would have had it done by now. You ought to be ashamed. You know better. What would_____ think if he/she knew? God, I am so stupid to let this pile up this way! This house looks like a pig sty!"

Here I go again, "telling off" on myself. This is a true story and continues to happen to this day.

I do not like to do filing in any shape, form or fashion. I think we ought to train chimpanzees to do our filing for us. It is a job that is boring, and besides that, I detest the paper cuts I get in my cuticles. (If you ever had a paper cut in the cuticle, you know how painful it is.) Because I detest filing, I would put the job off as long as possible. I would put it off so long that it would literally take me eight hours, one full working day, to complete my filing chore. While I was filing, what do you think I was saying to myself? "Patricia, if you had done just a little each day, you wouldn't have this pile of papers three feet high to do now." By the end of the eight hours, I was so tired - mentally, physically and emotionally - that it was all I could do to get into my car and go home. I had every intention of never doing it again, but what do you think happened again and again? And each time I put off filing, it seemed as if my piles got bigger. Believe me, I could come up with every excuse in the world why I did not need to file.

Today, I have an entirely different way of thinking about filing. I still do not like to file, and I still let it pile up. What has changed is how I think about filing. Now, when I file, instead of the blame/shame/guilt/anger game I used to play, I think of a reward I would like to have when I finish my filing chore.

I no longer think of putting off filing as procrastination. I consider it an "eccentricity". BUT(comma), I have only one "eccentricity". I no longer procrastinate on other chores.

Do you notice I keep using the word "chore"? Does the word "chore" have a negative or a positive emotion attached to it? What word can we change "chore" into? How does adventure sound? Or use any word you would like to use to make a job more exciting!

I am a firm believer in rewards. I have a reward jar. Into this reward jar I have written on pieces of paper the things I would like to do, which I would normally not take the time to do, i.e.

1. treating myself to a movie
2. feeding the ducks at the lake
3. window shopping
4. buying a new book
5. a drive into the country
6. a new video tape
7. going to a new restaurant

You get the idea. When I undertake one of my adventures in a timely manner, I reward myself from my reward jar.

Back to the filing:

While I am filing, I think about the rewards I have in my jar. I picture in my mind, drawing out that piece of paper and the pleasure I will have later treating myself. As I finish the filing, I am amazed at how quickly the challenge has gone. Instead of eight hours to complete the filing, it has only taken three.

At this point, how am I feeling? I have energy physically, mentally, and emotionally. I tell myself, " What a good job you have done Patricia and now you can treat yourself." Has this reward system built my self-esteem and self-confidence?

As soon as possible, I recommend within twenty-four hours, that you treat yourself to your reward. If you do not do it soon, you will find yourself reverting to old habits (procrastination).

By using this method for procrastination, you will find that you are procrastinating less and less. Rewards are different for everyone. Choose things you do infrequently. This helps build your anticipation. What kind of energy do you have when you are anticipating something pleasurable?

I will ask you again, why do we procrastinate? We procrastinate because we have a "chore" we do not like to do. If you were asked to go to the movies with a friend, go out to dinner, or spend the weekend at the shore, would you procrastinate?

How do we put a stop to procrastination? By changing our thoughts, perspective, and energy towards the "chore" in a positive and constructive manner. Find reasons to use your reward jar every day for one month. I promise you will see a definite improvement in your attitude towards "chores".

How many days does it take to form a new habit? Remember, the longer we use the new habit, the weaker the synaptic bridges become until the old habit disappears forever.

73

Remember, we must make the new habit stronger than the old habit if we are going to change our life; otherwise, we fall right back into that old habit!

EXERCISE FOR ELIMINATING PROCRASTINATION

1. Close your eyes.
2. Take several deep breathes to relax your body.
3. Go to your "Special Place".
4. Visualize your "Situation Room". See yourself procrastinating about a particular chore.
5. Enter into your "Rehearsal Room". Watch yourself performing that chore with energy and anticipation of your "Reward Jar". After the chore is completed, draw out that slip of paper with your reward on it.
6. Enter your "Goal Room". Experience everything you saw in your "Rehearsal Room". Luxuriate in the experience and the pleasure of your reward.
7. Open your eyes.

UNHEALTHY/UNHAPPY

Many unsuccessful people are unhealthy and unhappy. Have you ever heard of an unhealthy, happy person? (Of course not; I just wanted to be sure!)

How can we be healthy when we send out negative energy? This is truly impossible! Just as positive energy attracts positive energy, negative energy attracts negative energy.

When people are complaining about everything wrong in their lives, what kind of energy are they sending out with their thoughts? This negative energy affects our body.

What do doctors now say about stress? Stress affects everyone. Depending on each individual, stress will attack the weakest part of our body.

Doctors are now, in recent years, healing from a holistic point of view (body, brain and mind). The nursing profession, chiropractics, and other alternative health practitioners have always had a holistic viewpoint. They have known how important the mental attitude of the patient was for the patient to recover more quickly.

The body, brain, and mind need to work together under our conscious control. This is what you have been learning to do with your "Goal Room" exercises. You must learn to be in control of your thoughts at all times. It is the mind that is the controlling force which decides our future. The body only obeys whatever energy is directed to it.

Later in this book, we will discuss Energy Flow, so we can understand how and why energy affects us.

It is my belief that all of our illnesses (excluding AIDS, MAN-MADE VIRUSES, and genetic defects) are caused by what we think. Stress is the major cause of the majority of our illnesses.

In a previous exercise you have been shown how to control stress. With stress under control, you have alleviated the majority of your illnesses. You can become a healthy, happy individual. Unhealthy people focus their energy on what can go wrong or what is wrong with their lives. Healthy people focus on what they want to HAVE-BE-or-DO with their lives and how everything can go RIGHT!

Which are you? Do you have frequent problems with:

1. Headaches
2. Stomach aches
3. Heart
4. Allergies (sinus, hay fever)
5. Arthritis
6. Weight
7. Colds/flu
8. Colon
9. Drugs
10. Blood pressure

These are a few of the illnesses plaguing the American public today. These illnesses have grown to epic proportions over the last twenty years. Why? I believe it is due to not taking care of "self" and the fast pace of today's society. Everyone wants material possessions, especially those possessions that others have. This is okay, but I ask you, at what expense? You can have everything you want in life, including your health, by learning to use positive and constructive energy.

<u>Your number one job in life is to be in perfect health.</u>

If you are afflicted with constant health problems, such as the ones mentioned previously, and you have come to expect them, why are you surprised when these illnesses happen? Let me share another story with you from my childhood.

As a child, every year when winter came, I can remember my mother telling other people, "Well, Patricia always gets bronchitis at least twice a year. (Usually around Thanksgiving or Christmas, and then again in February or March) She is always out of school with each bout at least 2 weeks."

Guess what happened every year? Just like clockwork, I had bronchitis at least twice a year. Has this kind of occurrence been a part of your life? Perhaps it is "just" a headache that you have frequently.

WARNING! ANOTHER PERSONAL QUESTION AHEAD. Were you born into this world with headaches or any of the health problems you may have? If you were not born into this world with them, how were you so lucky to receive these wonderful gifts? (I hope you recognized facetiousness when you read it!)

You had to learn how to cause your affliction, over and over again, which caused the affliction to become a habit. If a headache is your problem, I would bet you that your headaches come at a particular time of day or with a particular set of circumstances. (I can remember as a child walking up to my mother and asking, "What's a headache? What does it feel like? Does it hurt very bad?") Learn to retrain your thoughts so your body is no longer afflicted with headaches.

76

Do you enjoy your poor health? If you do not, then change your health. Practice with the following exercise. I will use for my example a headache. It is important to remember, that when you feel a headache coming on, STOP what you are doing and go to my favorite room (the bathroom) to do this exercise. If you let the headache become full-blown, you will not be successful using this exercise. You might as well take your aspirins!

HEALTH EXERCISE

1. Close your eyes.
2. Take several deep breaths to relax the body.
3. Go to your "Special place" to relax the mind.
4. Enter the "Situation Room".
5. See yourself with the headache. Visualize the circumstances surrounding you which are causing you to create the headache. At this point, you know how you are feeling and what the stress is.
6. Enter your "Rehearsal Room".
7. Visualize yourself headache free. Feel yourself relaxing and handling whatever the situation/person is that has caused you to create the headache. You are able to continue with whatever you were doing, feeling absolutely wonderful and pain free!
8. Enter your "Goal Room". Experience everything you visualized in your second room.

You can use this exercise with any of your illnesses. With practice, you will learn to relax in any situation, so your body will OBEY you to create perfect health. With practice (Oh no, she is telling me to practice again!) you will become a healthy, happy person, being able to focus your energies on what you want in life.

If you are financially able, The Silva Method can help you further along your path to better health.

FEAR

What is fear? (Thought we were through with the dictionary, didn't you!) The dictionary's definition states that fear is:

"to feel a painful apprehension of, as some impending evil; to be afraid of; to dread ...to terrify; to expect with misgiving."

The dictionary's definition of fearful is:

:affected by fear; feeling fear; afraid ...showing or resulting from fear."

As far as the extent of my knowledge is concerned, there are only <u>two kinds</u> of fear. One is physical fear and the other is mental fear. Shall we talk about physical fear first? All right, I believe we will.

As usual, I will "<u>tell off</u>" on myself. As a young child, around the age of four or five, I remember my father telling me that I knew no fear and had never met a stranger. (I did not know what he meant at that time, but I believed him. Remember children think inductively until the age of six or seven.) I had to be taught to be wary of strangers, to look out for traffic before walking out into the street, and other normal everyday things that children need to be taught due to their age.

I truly never comprehended what fear was. I never **learned** fear at an early age. I did the things I was told to do because I was supposed to and I knew Daddy wouldn't tell me something that would hurt me. I used to climb trees, play with all sorts of reptiles (including garden snakes), climb out my upstairs window onto the roof of our home, and ride my bicycle like a bat out of ____. I would talk to any of my parents' friends as if they were my friends.

Later, in my teenage years, I realized all of a sudden that I WAS AFRAID OF SNAKES AND HEIGHTS!!! Can you guess from whom I learned the fear? My mother. My mother is deathly afraid of snakes, heights, and enclosed places. She was constantly telling me why I should be afraid of heights and snakes until I took on her fear as my own. (Not to say that <u>her</u> fears were not valid!) Fear of heights and snakes became a reality for me. It wasn't until a few years ago I was able to desensitize

79

myself to heights and snakes. Now, don't misunderstand me; if you fall from a great height, chances are you are going to be hurt. One should always be <u>aware</u> of one's surroundings, but my fear had grown to the point that I could not go up in an elevator to the upper floors of a tall building, especially those with glass elevators.

The majority of the snakes where I grew up were rattlers, water moccasins, and copperheads. All of these snakes are poisonous, <u>but my mind</u> did not stop with those; it included <u>all</u> snakes. (If having these fears were not bad enough, when you tell someone, they laugh at you and say, "You shouldn't be afraid of _____," or "That is silly. You are an adult and should know better. There is nothing to be afraid of.")

How cruel others can be! Who are "they" anyway, telling me that I shouldn't be afraid or how I should be feeling. Do they think we receive pleasure from our fears? Or that we have a dial, and we can turn our fear off and on at our leisure? The fears I have been sharing with you are physical fears that I made larger in my mind. With reasonable precautions, I can be safe from heights and snakes.

Instead, what did I allow to happen? I built the fear in my mind to such a large proportion that when thinking about either snakes or heights, the fear would paralyze me. I thought of every negative circumstance that <u>could</u> occur instead of the reasonable precautions I could take to <u>prevent the circumstances from occurring</u>.

What is all of this leading to? The point I am making is that fear pertaining to the physical body is a normal, natural, and a healthy occurrence. Part of our brain is called the primordial brain. This is the first part of the brain that is developed in a human being. The primordial brain's job is the "fight or flight" mechanism. When you are frightened, the primordial brain takes over conscious reasoning. It triggers the adrenal glands to pump the hormone adrenalin directly into the blood system. The purpose of adrenalin in this case is to make the muscles stronger so that we can avoid danger.

All of us have heard stories of a 100 pound woman, seeing her husband pinned under an automobile, lifts the automobile off her husband. Would this woman normally have been able to achieve this super action?

No, the primordial brain took over conscious reasoning to help this woman perform this amazing action by releasing adrenalin into her system to make her stronger. The "flight or fight" mechanism pumps up our muscles with adrenalin, then conscious reasoning returns and we have the choice to FIGHT or to RUN.

Another example of the "fight or flight mechanism" is if someone tries to start a fist fight with you. You are immediately filled with adrenalin. Your conscious reasoning returns and you have to decide if you are going to fight them or turn around and walk away (personally, I would run VERY FAST. I am not into pain, mine or theirs!). If someone points a gun at me, I am going to be afraid! (In fact, I am going to be afraid all the way down my legs, creating a puddle on the floor!) When the physical body is threatened, you are supposed to be afraid.

But fear built out of proportion in the mind is neither normal or natural. Fear of this nature is called a phobia. How was this phobia created? You created it. You learned it.

Patricia, you have to be wrong. Why would I want to LEARN fear? Because it is acceptable in our society to be afraid except when that fear turns into a "phobia". Then society turns on us and says that it is not acceptable any longer, but by this time it is too late for us. The phobia is created and we believe we are "stuck" with it. That is not so!!! Would you like to learn how to "get rid" of any phobia? (I am assuming you said yes.)

RED ALERT! Here comes another nosy question!!! Did your fear start out "full-blown", or did it grow gradually? In other words, did it start out as big as a mountain or as small as a mole hill? You can and will learn to eliminate the fear the same way you learned to create it. Let's use claustrophobia for my example.

EXERCISE FOR PHOBIAS

1. Close your eyes.
2. Take several deep breaths to relax the body.
3. Mentally go to your "Special place" to relax your mind.
4. Create your "Situation Room".

In this room, see yourself experiencing your claustrophobia (I will use a closet for the exercise).

You are inside the closet, the door is closed, and the closet is dark. Clothes are hanging down, touching your body. There is no fresh air. You are unable to breathe. You are so frightened that you are unable to speak or move. (Remember, you are looking at yourself as if you were watching a movie.)
5. Visualize the door and see yourself enter your "Rehearsal Room".

This is where we are going to desensitize ourselves, step-by-step.

Imagine or visualize a closet in this room. There is no door on this closet. This closet is well lit with no switch to turn off the light. Clothes are hanging in this closet. You KNOW that they are your clothes, and it is totally safe for you because this is your imagination, and nothing in the physical world can harm you. Walk towards the closet, enter the closet, turn around and walk out of the closet. Once you are in the center of your room, turn around and look at the closet. There is still no door on the closet. The lights are on; it still has your clothes hanging in it, and you are still completely safe and secure. Now congratulate yourself. Tell yourself how easy and comfortable you were or any other PRAISE you need.

If at any time you need to open your eyes during the exercise to reassure yourself that you are indeed safe, do so. Reassure yourself that you are in control, safe, and comfortable; then close your eyes and resume the exercise.

6. Go to the third door and enter your "Goal Room".

As you know, in this third room you will experience everything that you created in the second room.

You are feeling safe, relaxed, and comfortable. You see that there is no door to the closet, and the lights are on with no off switch. The clothes hanging in the closet are yours, and you know every item. There is plenty of air circulating in the closet. You are able to breathe normally and naturally with great ease. You walk into the closet, turn around, and walk out again. When you are in the center of the room again, you turn around, looking at the closet, and praise yourself on how well you behaved, feeling relaxed, comfortable, safe, and in control.

7. Open your eyes.

Practice this exercise until you feel that you are completely relaxed, safe, comfortable and in control. Remember, when practicing this exercise, we only want to practice with the second and third rooms. We already know how the first room feels, and we want to give energy **only** to the second and third rooms, which are our desired end results.

Your next exercise, after becoming comfortable with this first exercise, might be:

1. Adding a door to the closet, or
2. Lowering the lights in closet, or
3. Standing in the closet for a longer period of time, or
4. Closing the door with the lights on, or
5. Repeating steps 2,3, or 4 with the lights lowered, or
6. Turning off the light in the closet with the door open, or
7. Repeating step 3 with step 6, and eventually
8. Closing the door to the closet with the lights out

Do whatever you feel is necessary and take as many steps as you feel are necessary for you to become desensitized. Each of the steps, 1 through 8, are to be added to the exercise above, one at a time when you feel comfortable with adding them.

Take a moment to go back into your past. Approximately how many years did it take for you to form a phobia? It will take considerably less time, by many years, for you to become desensitized.

It took me a little over a year before I could touch a snake. Snakes are not one of my favorite creatures. But now I have the choice to either stay in the same room or leave. I am not motivated by fear but through conscious reasoning and the freedom of choice. Do you remember the dictionary's definition of fear? Fear is:

"to expect with misgivings"

You have come to **expect** to be afraid. When you have desensitized your phobias, how do you **expect** to feel? Winston Churchill once said, "There is nothing to fear but fear itself."

Hopefully, you are now able to comprehend that the majority of the things we "fear" are created and built in the mind. Other than the two fears I have mentioned (whether I had the good sense or not), I have never been afraid of anyone or anything. You can achieve the same success and peace of mind. But to achieve that success and peace of mind, what do you have to do? (You can scream now because I am going to say it again!)

PRACTICE, PRACTICE, PRACTICE!

How do you expect to be a successful human being when you are fearful? With this exercise you can become fear-less. What is the opposite of fearful?

COURAGEOUS

ANGER

From my own experience, I believe anger to be one of the most negative and limiting traits a person can have. Why do I believe that anger is a limiting and negative trait? Because we usually tend to focus on the anger of a situation, letting the anger turn into rage. We are emotional human beings. We are allowed to have and experience anger, but we are not allowed to let that anger turn into rage which in turn immobilizes us, and keeps us from making good choices in our lives.

Let's look at the dictionary's definition of anger:

> *"A strong feeling excited by real or supposed injury; often accompanied by a desire to take vengeance, or to obtain satisfaction from the offending party; resentment; wrath; ire... pain or trouble."*

I do not know about you, but I do not like what I have just read. Let's take the definition apart, word for word.

> *"A **strong** feeling excited by **REAL** or **SUPPOSED** injury."*

I believe we could take that to mean a strong feeling caused by hurt inflicted by words or deeds. Do you agree?

> *"Often accompanied by a **desire to take vengeance**"*

Would this mean to retaliate because of what has been said or done to us?

> *"Or to **obtain satisfaction** from the offending party"*

Could this satisfaction be by returning hurt by word or deed, or seeking an apology from the offender?

> *"Resentment; wrath; ire;...pain or trouble."*

Isn't it amazing all the negative words, emotions, and deeds that arise from the word "anger"?

I also have my own definition of the word anger. I believe we get angry when we are not able to:

"control" what others are saying or how they are acting.

Stop and think about the last time you got angry. Wasn't someone saying or doing something you did not like? Didn't you want them to say or do what you wanted? In other words, to agree with you? Isn't that called "controlling" others?

I would like to share the following story with you.

You are in an excellent mood this morning. You got up on time, the kids got off to school with no hassles, and everything seemed to flow smoothly. As you are driving to work, some "Jerk" cuts you off, barely missing you by inches!

What is your reaction? Well, you have more than one reaction. Let's examine them one by one.

1. fear - fight or flight mechanism takes over
2. relief - no accident
3. anger - action of the driver
4. rage - continuing to think about the situation

Your first reaction is fear. The primordial brain takes over and pumps adrenalin into your system. Your conscious reasoning takes over from the primordial brain and tells you that you cannot fight, and in this instance running is not appropriate either. The "Jerk" has gone on his merry way.

Now is when <u>you need to take a deep breath</u> and realize, with relief, that you are all right, and no accident has occurred. Now you get angry. HOW DARE that so-n-so cut you off like that and scare you half to death!

Let's look at the situation. Apply my definition of anger to the above situation. Aren't you angry because you could not control that "Jerk" from cutting in front of you and scaring you half to death?

Five minutes from now, do you think that "Jerk" will remember cutting you off? Does the "Jerk" **KNOW** that you are **ANGRY**? Does the "Jerk" **CARE**? If you continue to be angry, who has YOUR CONTROL, you or the "**Jerk**"?

Let's continue with the story.

When you arrive at work, you see one of your co-workers, and you proceed to tell them what the "Jerk" did.

This incident happened twenty minutes ago, but you are still angry and getting angrier by the minute.

At lunch time, you proceed to tell another employee what happened to you on the way to work that morning.

By this time, your anger is turning into extreme anger.

At 4:30 pm you are getting ready to go home, and again you tell another employee what occurred that morning, and boy do you hope you see that "Jerk" again.

Now your anger has turned into rage!

At 5:00 pm when it is time for me to go home, I do not want to get into my car. I want a SHERMAN TANK to drive home in! No wonder we have people being driven off the roads. No wonder when someone makes an obscene gesture, the person the gesture has been directed to, pulls out a gun and shoots the person that made the obscene gesture! Perhaps some "Jerk" cut in front of them that morning and they have had all they can tolerate. Their rage is out of control!

What is the dictionary's definition of rage?

*"to show **violent** anger in <u>action</u> or <u>speech</u>."*

We must, for our own sake and the safety of others, learn to release our anger in a healthy manner. Several good self-help books have been written on the subject of anger. If you are unable to examine why you are angry, and you are unable to release the anger, I suggest you go to your favorite book store and purchase a book on anger or find a therapist that specializes in dealing with anger.

We have three choices we can make when we are angry. We can:

1. walk away from the situation
2. change our perspective of the situation
3. accept the situation

Back to the "Jerk" that cut us off. How can we release our anger in a healthy manner?

1. Take several deep breaths to relax the body from the adrenalin rush.
2. Out loud, tell yourself that you are safe.
3. Out loud, tell yourself that you are in control.

4. Out loud, tell yourself that yes you are
   angry because of the "Jerk's" reckless driving.
5. Out loud, tell yourself that you have chosen
   to release the anger.
6. Put a smile on your face and thank the
   Universe that you are safe, secure, and in control.
7. DO NOT REPEAT the story to anyone else. When you repeat the
   story YOU continue to give negative energy and negative emotions
   to it. This is part of letting the anger go!

Which of our three options have you chosen to take? You have decided to change your perspective of the situation. You cannot change what happened nor can you walk away from it because the event is in the past. You have changed your perspective by changing your <u>reaction</u> to the situation. You are **acting** instead of **reacting**!

The following is an exercise for releasing anger.

EXERCISE FOR RELEASING ANGER

1. Close your eyes.
2. Take several deep breaths to relax the body.
3. Go to your "Special place" to relax the mind.
4. In the "Situation Room" replay in your mind the situation that made you angry.
5. Enter the "Rehearsal Room" and examine what was said or done that you did not like? Now examine yourself to see why you would control someone to speak or act as you would have them do. How can you change how you are feeling about this anger?
6. Enter you "Goal Room". Experience releasing the anger in the manner you have chosen in your "Rehearsal Room". ALWAYS REMEMBER, you can accept or reject what others say or do.
7. Decide which of the three choices you are going to make to help you release your anger.
   A. walk away from the situation
   B. change your perspective of the situation
   C. accept the situation as it is
8. Make your changes then open your eyes, feeling relaxed and in control.

Are others allowed to have their opinions or thoughts? Would you appreciate it if someone tried to control how you speak and act? I am not saying you have to like what others say or do, but do you have the right to control others (parents I am speaking of other adults, not your children)? Who, in the book of life, made you the judge and jury?

88

And for the younger folks who might be reading this book, can't you walk away from others your age if you don't like what they are saying or doing? Of course you can. If you do this, your peers might realize that their behavior is not acceptable to you, and their actions might also change in a positive and constructive way towards others. Haven't your previous actions been influenced by your friends?

I find when I get angry with someone, there is usually a change I need to make. It is like holding up a mirror, and I do not like the reflection I am seeing. Perhaps you might consider this when working on your anger.

Another suggestion I might pass along is: when you are not able to get a "hold" on your anger, tell the person that you are angry and that you need to leave the room. Call a **TIME OUT**. When you are in control and can talk calmly about the situation, you will return and continue the discussion.

When has anger ever truly achieved the results you wanted (other than the momentary pleasure of revenge)? Is anger physically , mentally, spiritually, and emotionally draining? How can you use your energy for better results? By practicing (there's that word again) the exercise for releasing anger.

DENIAL

To discover the definition of denial, we must look at the word "deny". The dictionary's definition of deny is:

"to declare to be untrue... to disavow; to disown; to withhold."

The dictionary's definition of denial is:

"the act of denying; a flat contradiction; a refusal."

How can we ever become a successful human being if we continually deny that we have a problem or problems? Can you relate to any of the following:

1. fear
2. negativity
3. poor health
4. procrastination
5. addiction(s) (drugs, alcohol, sex, food, gambling, etc)
6. dishonesty
7. gossiping/spreading rumors
8. ethics (business and personal)
9. morals (business and personal)
10. Abuse

How can we solve a problem whenever we continually deny we have a problem?

Well, Patricia, what you consider to be a problem I might have may not be considered to be a problem by me! GRANTED! It is not my job to judge you nor is it anyone else's job. But, (I am famous for my but commas, which I borrowed from a good friend of mine, Marlene Skapura) if it were not for others bringing to my attention (in a loving manner) things that I might need to look at and consider changing and working on, otherwise I might not have known I needed to make some changes.

The following is my yardstick for judging if there are "possible" changes that I might need to address. When two or more people call to my attention the same thing, I stop and seriously examine what has been said. Nine times out of ten, it is something I need to change. I will give you an example:

> When I am at work, I tend to totally focus and concentrate on my job to the exclusion of everyone around me. I believe this is what I am being paid to do. I am friendly with everyone, but I focus on my job. One day, three different people asked me if I was having a bad day. I was absolutely astonished at being asked the same question by three different people. I asked the last person why he thought I was having a bad day. His reply was, "Because I haven't seen you smile all day." I could very easily have gone into denial by stating that I had smiled several times that day, but instead I took their "constructive criticism" and made a conscious effort to smile at people the rest of the day.

What possible good would it have done me to argue or deny that I had smiled that day. They were just not around when I had done so. Sometimes we tend to become defensive when there is no need. Twenty years ago I might - no more than "might" - I know I would have taken their statements defensively or felt like I was being attacked or being "picked on".

With the self-ness work (self-ness is becoming aware and taking care of self) I have been actively working on everyday, I am able to look at myself honestly, without feeling threatened by other's statements or actions. Don't get me wrong; I still have a few "buttons" that can be pushed, but those are "buttons" I am aware of and continuously work on every day.

One of my favorite expressions comes from one of John Bradshaw's seminars. "We need to learn to be a human being, instead of a human doing." I am learning to be a human being, not a human doing. He also coined the word "self-ness". Thank you John.

Another way I can determine when I am in denial is that I discover that I feel as if I am running away mentally from a situation and not facing up to whatever it is I need to take care of. Or, I find myself trying to convince others that whatever has been said or done is emphatically NOT SO!!! These particular situations are my silent "alarms" that warn me when I need to sit down and take a serious look at whatever it is I am denying.

I think I need to mention at this time that it is not your job to judge or criticize the actions, words, or deeds of others unless you are on a jury. When you start taking care of self, you will not have time to judge or criticize others. Do you like to be criticized or judged by others, especially by people that do not know you?

I learned many years ago that unsolicited opinions and advice are not taken kindly. At this stage in my life, I only give my opinion or advice when I am asked.

Hopefully you can learn this lesson at an earlier age than I. Believe me, it will save you a lot of heartache in the future if you learn this lesson sooner, rather than later.

Denial is one of the biggest factors in keeping you where and who you are instead of where and who you want to be. Denial can be:

SNEAKY, SMUG, BLIND, AND INSIDIOUS

Denial influences every part of our life. Learn to recognize denial in all its "forms". Only by recognizing denial can we change our lives into what we want to become.

EXERCISE FOR ELIMINATING DENIAL

1. Close your eyes.
2. Take several deep breathes to relax the body.
3. Visualize your "Special place" to relax your mind.
4. In the "Situation Room" remember someone telling you about something you need to change and your denial of the change.
5. Enter the "Rehearsal Room". See the above situation and you are deciding what you need to do to make the change. You have made your choice and are visualizing the steps you need to take to make your change.
6. Enter your "Goal Room" and experience the steps you have chosen to make your change and how comfortable you are with the change. You know this is the right choice because it "feels right".
7. Open your eyes.

How are you feeling now that you have made a positive and constructive change in your life?

"WHAT IF/IF ONLY"

Rest your fingers and brain for this chapter because there are no trips to the dictionary. YEAH! That is, I am assuming you have been looking in the dictionary, if for no other reason than to see if I am using the correct definitions and that by now, hopefully, you possibly trust me just a little and have stopped looking up the definitions. I can hear some of you kids saying "NOT"!

Oh yes, back to the subject of this chapter. Many times in my life I have said, "What if I had only done this", or "If I had only said that." I hear these statements from others on a daily basis. The most common ones I hear are:

1. "If only I had been born as pretty as you..."
2. "If only I had gone to college I would be a..."
3. "If only I had been born rich I would..."
4. "What if I had done this instead of..."
5. "What if I change, will you..."

I call people that make these statements "what if'ers" or "if onlys". These people live their lives in the past. They do not take responsibility for self. Whatever the reason or reasons they may think they have, in their eyes it is easier for them to stay where they are and to place the blame on others.

It is much easier for you to blame and point the finger at others for your "lack of" than taking responsibility for changing the way you are. Remember, when you point your finger at others, how many fingers are pointing back at you?

We should have been taught that we remember the past for only one reason. We remember the past so we can learn from our mistakes, and not to "wallow" in those mistakes for self pity or the sympathy of others or as an excuse for not achieving what we want in life. What has blaming others for your situation ever achieved? Absolutely nothing except the above!

Energy flows in a circle, remember? You have to get out of the "guilt, shame, blame game" if you ever want to better your life. What keeps returning to you and keeps getting bigger? The negative energy you have sent out.

It requires positive time, energy, effort, and practice to better your life. If deep in your heart, you want what others have, then use your "Goal Room" to help you achieve this. <u>Don't blame others</u> for what you **don't have**. It is **your responsibility** to attract the things to you that you want in life by using **positive thoughts and energy**.

The only time I consider "What if" to be valid is when I am exploring the possibilities of finding the correct solution to a problem. "What if" seems to help my creativity. For example:

What if I choose this solution instead of this one? What are the consequences with this particular choice? Of my choices, <u>which is</u> the better solution?

Quit playing the "What if, if only" game. You cannot change the past with "What if, if only" but you can change your future by not repeating the same mistake. Use your "Goal Room" exercise to change your "What if, if only's".

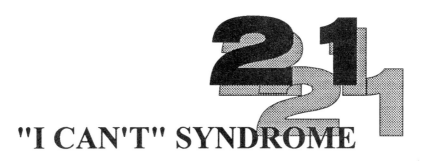

"I CAN'T" SYNDROME

"I can't." These three words, of all the words in the English language, keep you from becoming, having, or doing whatever it is you want in life. "I can't" is socially acceptable. We have learned to use "I can't" almost from birth. First of all, there is nothing in this world you cannot do if you choose to do it and if it is on your list of priorities. You have only one limitation and that is physically.

For instance, if you have brown eyes, can you physically change your eye color? (no contacts allowed.) If you are an adult and have been 5'2" all of your life, can you grow an extra four inches and become 5'6"? (no high heels.) These are physical limitations. Your DNA decided your eye color and your height.

Other than these physical limitations, you CAN do anything you CHOOSE to do in life. You do have choice and free will. If you want something in life, how much of your (oh no, not again) time, energy, effort, and practice are you willing to invest in achieving your desired end results?

As children, we are told what we can or cannot do. The majority of these "can'ts" are for our protection. But, we soon learn to use these "I can'ts" because of:

1. FEAR
2. LAZINESS
3. AS AN EXCUSE

I call the "I can'ts" a syndrome. We use "I can't" so often in our daily life that the majority of the time we do not realize that we are saying it, nor do we realize the end results of "I can't".

From whom did we learn to use "I can't"? Everyone! We learned this limitation as children. Here is another story to illustrate one "possible" way we could have learned "I can't". Perhaps you or your children have experienced this situation.

There is a child approximately four to five years of age. Recently, she has been shown how to tie her shoes. This is her responsibility from now on. She knows how to tie her shoes, and before she can go outside to play, she must tie her shoes. One day she decides to go outside. She remembers that she <u>must</u> tie her shoes. At this point, she knows it will take her five minutes to tie one shoe and five minutes to tie the other shoe, and before she can get to the door, they will become untied.

Children are very smart. Why should she keep having to retie her shoes when Mommy or Daddy can tie them, and they will stay tied?

So, off she runs to Daddy and says, "Daddy, please tie my shoes." Daddy replies, "Now, Patricia, you know how to tie your shoes. We have shown you." The little girl looks up at her Daddy, chin quivering, tear drops in each eye, and says, "But Daddy, I can't." And what do you promptly do? You reach down and tie her shoes!

What have you just done? You have taught your child "learned helplessness". I know you tied the shoes out of kindness, but what are the end results in the child's life?

We continue through life using "I can't". "I Can't" is learned helplessness. "Learned helplessness" is:

1. FEAR
2. LAZINESS
3. AN EXCUSE

Soon we truly do (through making "I can't" a habit) fear the unknown, learn to be lazy, or just use it as an excuse not to do something.

The following story is another way YOU help perpetuate the "I can't" syndrome. (Hum, I wonder if this example is possibly something you might have done.)

You are at work. Several projects need to be completed before 5 pm. You notice a fellow employee is not busy, so you walk over and ask them to help you. The first words out of their mouth are "I can't; I don't know how." A look of disbelief comes over your face, and you reply, "Well, never mind; I will do it myself!"

Have you perpetuated "learned helplessness"? In my opinion you have. If you are not willing to show someone "how to" so they "can", you allow the "I can't" syndrome to continue. Take "a little time" on your part to help build someones' self-esteem and self-confidence. There is also a bonus for you in doing this. Don't you <u>feel</u> <u>better</u> when you have helped someone else?

Let me share another example with you from my life. I am a "permanent" temporary. I work forty hours a week for a temporary agency. Let's pretend you are calling an agency for a temporary.

You need a person with word processing skills on WordPerfect. I have worked on several software packages but not this particular one. When I walk in the door, the first question you ask me is if I have experience with WordPerfect. I reply that I do not have experience with WordPerfect, and I do not think I can use it.

What would be the first thing **you** would do? You would probably get on the phone to the agency to have me replaced. But, what if I made this reply instead?

"No, I do not have experience with WordPerfect but I know I can if someone will show me.

How do you feel about these statements? I believe you would give me a chance because of the positive way I replied. With further questioning you would discover that I had experience on MicrosoftWord or some other word processing package.

How long would I be a temporary if I made negative statements as in the first example? I enjoy being a temporary because I like change. Once I have learned my job, I am ready to move on to something new. Plus I enjoy meeting new people.

In the computer field, new software is developed on a daily basis. If I stayed with one employer, I would miss all the new "stuff" and experiences I gain working with different types of companies.

I am sure you have heard this adage before, "<u>Can't</u> never did anything." True, so true! If you do not know how to do something, read a book or ask someone to help you. There will always be someone around <u>who can</u> show you. So...which person are you going to be, an "I can" or an "I can't"?

Is there something you have always wanted to do but are always being told you "can't" do it? Perhaps it is because you are:

1. a woman
2. too old
3. financially unable
4. inexperienced
5. without proper education

It is sad to say, but other people sometimes make these statements because they failed and do not wish to see others succeed. Are you willing to accept other people's limitations? Do you want to be a carbon copy of their failures? Remember, you can do anything you want in life if:

1. YOU CHOOSE TO DO IT, and
2. IF IT IS ON YOUR LIST OF PRIORITIES.

I am going to use a hypothetical situation for my next example.

Suppose at this time in my life, I have decided to become a doctor. I am very happy with my decision and want to share this with my friends and family. The first obstacles I encounter are:

1. "You can't do that; you are too old."
2. "Do you realize how old you will be when you finish?"
3. "Do you know how much money it takes for medical school?"
4. "How can you afford it?"
5. "Are you out of your mind?"
6. "You're not serious!"
7. "Whatever possessed you to think you can become a doctor?"
8. "Do you realize the hours involve in medical school, then your Internship, and then your residency?"

After this barrage of negativity from family and friends, is it any wonder that I might change my mind and doubt myself? Isn't it wonderful the way they have helped to build my self-esteem and self-confidence?

The situations like the above truly sadden me. What is worse is that you listen and believe what others have said to you. If you truly want something badly enough, you will ignore their comments. You will find the time, energy, and effort to achieve what you want. YOU CAN have whatever you want in life.

Be careful. You have used "I can't" for so many years that it rolls off of your tongue "like melted butter". You will say "I can't" before you realize you have said it.

I found an immediate turnaround in my life when I changed three words into two words. I changed "I can't" into "I CAN". I may not have the immediate knowledge I need, but I can find the person with the knowledge to teach me so **I CAN**.

You might want to make this one of your personal goals.

I CAN DO ANYTHING I CHOOSE

(Wow! This must be really important; she capitalized, bolded, and underlined it!)

With conscious effort, practice saying this as often as possible for twenty-one days. I promise you, YOU will see a definite difference in the results you will have in your life. It is almost like a miracle!

SUMMARY

Chapters Fourteen through Twenty-One are just a few traits of a negative person. There are many others that could be added to the list. I believe all of these traits stem from a lack of self-esteem and self-confidence. Take a serious and honest look at your life. Is it everything you want it to be? Are you attracting the situations and people into your life that you want? Are you successful or unsuccessful?

Which kind of person are you? No matter what your age, you CAN change your life. You can succeed in any area of your life by using the "Goal Room" exercises.

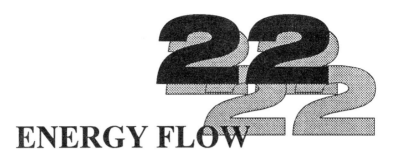

ENERGY FLOW

In a previous chapter I mentioned that we would discuss how our mental energy operates. But first, let me ask you a question. What is a "Universal Law"? The first time I was asked this question, I went totally blank! I had never heard of a "Universal Law". Let me explain. A "Universal Law" is a law that effects everyone on the planet the same way, no matter where they are.

Now, can you think of a "Universal Law" that affects everyone on the planet the same way, no matter what their location? Gravity, of course! You can be in Moscow, Dallas, at the North Pole, or at the South Pole. Gravity will affect you. This is a physical law that is also a "Universal Law".

Let's discuss a mental law. We know from physics and science that energy flows in a circle. Have you ever heard the saying, "What goes around, comes around"? How often have you heard this saying? Was it quoted in a positive or a negative fashion? For example:

> Someone has taken advantage of you in an unfair manner. You are telling a friend about the incident, and you are very hurt and angry about it. Your last statement to your friend is, "Boy, would I like to be there when he/she gets his/hers. You know, what goes around, comes around!"

We know from previous chapters that our thoughts are energy. We also know that energy flows in a circle. We are able, as human beings, to renew our energy, which we pull into us from the Universe. Energy is neither negative or positive. Energy is pure and clean. Energy is changed to negative or positive by our thoughts. The following is an example of using energy in a negative or positive manner.

> You have come to visit me. While we are talking, I discover that you have not eaten today and are very hungry. I have a wonderful machine in my kitchen called a microwave oven. I plug this microwave oven into an electrical outlet. I prepare a meal for you.

Was this machine used for a positive or a negative purpose? It was used in a positive manner to prepare a meal for a hungry friend.

After you have eaten, I invite you into my living room to sit in a very "special" chair. This chair has metal arm straps, metal leg straps, and a metal helmet. I can also plug this "special" chair into an electrical outlet.

WOULD YOU LIKE TO SIT IN MY VERY SPECIAL "ELECTRIC" CHAIR?

Is this "special" chair to be used for a positive or negative purpose? I don't know about you, but I would not want to sit in an "ELECTRIC CHAIR"!

Does the electricity or energy coming from the electrical outlet know for what purpose it is to be used? Does the energy care? No, to both questions!

We, with our thoughts, have choice. **We, with our thoughts, can decide how to use our mental energy.** We can use our energy for positive or negative purposes. What all of the above is leading to is that we receive our energy pure and clean and we must return the energy in the same manner (when we are through with it), pure and clean.

Would you like to know how we channel energy into our bodies? We channel energy from the Universe through the top of our heads. (See illustration 1)

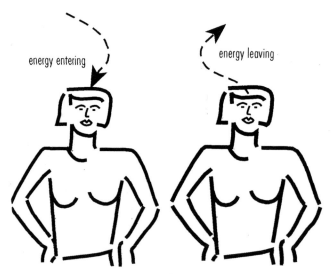

energy entering

energy leaving

illustration 1

104

The energy then fills the body and leaves through the center of the forehead. Since our thoughts are energy, and energy flows in a circle, what we send out comes back to us as in illustration #2.

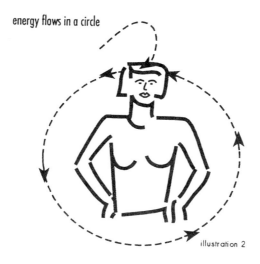

energy flows in a circle

illustration 2

The following are two examples of negative thoughts. Which statement has the most energy or power?

1. I just hate you. You wear some of the cutest clothes I have ever seen!
2. I HATE YOU! You are one of the meanest and most foul-mouthed persons I have ever met in my life.

Statement number two is the strongest. This statement was made with a lot of power behind the words. It will come back to us very quickly, probably within minutes due to the energy behind the words.

In statement number one, we really meant this as a compliment, didn't we? What is the one word that turned this sentence into a negative statement? HATE. Hate is the most <u>negative</u> word we can use in the English language. In statement number one, was there a lot of power behind it? Very little, if any!

The next illustrations show you how energy grows while it is out in the Universe.

Because the hate "thought" was so small when you sent it out, it will stay out in the Universe for a long time. (See illustration 3)

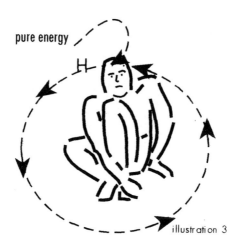

pure energy

illustration 3

While the energy is out in the Universe, the energy will attract to it more negative energy. The energy begins to grow and gain momentum. (See illustration 4)

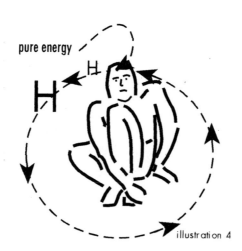

pure energy

illustration 4

As the negative energy grows, it attracts more negative energy to it. (See illustration 5)

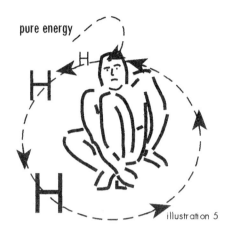

illustration 5

The energy is becoming more powerful now, and because it is more powerful, it attracts more negative energy to it. (See illustration 6)

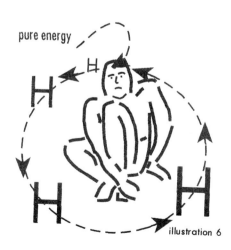

illustration 6

Because this "itsy-bitsy" negative thought has been out in the Universe, most likely for years, by the time it returns to you, the energy can almost literally knock you "off of your feet"! (See illustration 7)

pure energy

illustration 7

       Compare this energy to a snowball on top of a mountain. What happens when we push the snowball off the top of a mountain? The snowball starts moving down the mountain very slowly until it attracts more snow to it. It then becomes bigger and more powerful. How big and powerful is the snowball when it reaches the bottom of the mountain? It could destroy anything in its path, could it not?

       If you agree with this analogy, what happens to you when your "snowballed' negative energy returns to you? How does it affect you?

       STORY TIME! Has this ever happened to you?

       You seem to finally have you life "on track". The job is going well. Your personal life is just the way "you want it". You are able to save some money. The children are doing well in school. BUT, all of a sudden, out of nowhere, totally out of the blue, "something" happens, and it feels as if your world is falling apart, or the "rug" has just been pulled out from under you! You look up into the sky and say, "Why me? What did I do to deserve this?"

       I will tell you what you did to "deserve" this. It was one of those "itsy-bitsy" negative thoughts you sent out years ago that has just now returned to you.

108

Is this negative energy pure and clean? Can you return this kind of energy to the Universe the way it is? How are we going to change this negative energy?

We are going to filter this energy with our "bodies". Whoa, Patricia! What bodies are you talking about? I thought I only had one body. No, we have seven bodies. They are the:

1. physical body
2. mental body
3. emotional body
4. intellectual body
5. spiritual body
6. ethereal body
7. polar body

These seven bodies make up who we are as a human being. With all seven bodies we will filter the negative energy, so we can return the energy to the Universe pure and clean, just as we received it. I will be discussing only the first five bodies. I will leave the sixth and seventh bodies for another book! (But, if you are really interested, read The Kybalion by The Three Initiates.)

Since we know that negative energy is not pure and clean, what happens to our bodies (as we have to use all of them to filter this negative energy)? What can we expect? (See illustration 8)

pure energy

illustration 8

illness   poor health

poverty   troubles

problems

LACK OF

We can expect a "LACK OF" everything we need or want in life. This can lead to:

1. illness/poor health
2. poverty
3. troubles
4. problems
5. failures
6. a "LACK OF"

Can our bodies be affected by illness, problems and troubles etc.?

1. physical body - diseases
2. mental body - disorders
3. emotional body - no control over emotions
4. intellectual body - unable to learn/forgetfulness
5. spiritual body - lack of illumination/enlightenment

How many negative thoughts have you sent out in the past? How many have you sent out today? How many are still out in the Universe and have not returned to you? Can you do anything to change or stop negative thoughts? Before I answer that question, I believe I will let you think about it for "awhile".

Let's continue with the following two examples of positive thoughts.

1. I love your new car. I wish I had one just like it.
2. I LOVE YOU. Thank you for being my friend. You have always been here for me whenever I have needed you. I LOVE YOU.

Of the two examples, which is the most powerful with the most energy? Number two. Number one has the least amount of energy. But what word made number one a positive thought? LOVE! Number two is the stronger and more powerful and will more than likely return to you very quickly, again, probably within minutes, as it did with the stronger negative energy thought.

Number two is positive energy, or a love thought in this instance, which starts out small and continues to grow larger. The energy gathers more momentum the longer it is out in the Universe, as in illustrations 9 - 13. When this positive energy returns, will we need to filter it with our bodies? Is this energy pure and clean? Yes and Yes. Can you imagine your sense of well being when one of these love thoughts returns to you?

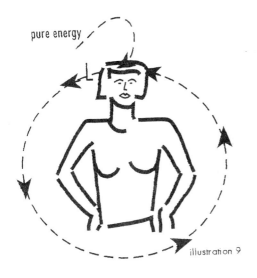

pure energy

illustration 9

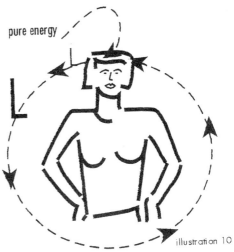

pure energy

illustration 10

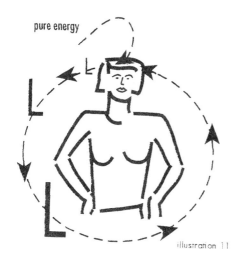

pure energy

illustration 11

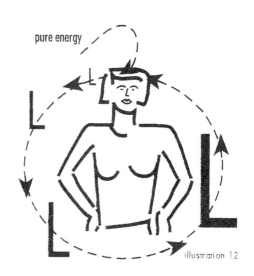

pure energy

illustration 12

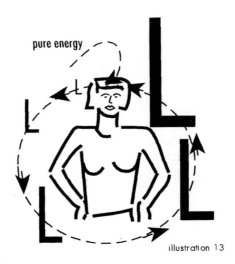

pure energy

illustration 13

This next story happened when one of my positive thoughts came back to me, just when I needed it the most!

I woke up late one morning for work and I could not decide what I wanted to wear; I burned my toast, had a flat tire, and arrived at work an hour-and-a-half late. The rest of the day seemed to go uphill from there. Remember Murphy's law? (What can go wrong, will go wrong!) I remember saying to myself, "What else can go wrong?". The Universe continued to show me, all day long, "what else could go wrong".

*It seemed like everything else DID go wrong. I received **exactly** what I **expected** by the negative thoughts I chose to think.*

Later that afternoon, a friend stopped me in the hallway. She wanted to tell me a joke. (By this time was I in any mood to listen to a joke?) Because I was in a rotten mood, I snapped at her and told her in no uncertain terms that I had no time to listen to a stupid joke. She continued to nag me until I finally, with no patience left, listened to her joke. The joke was rather long, and I found that I was becoming wrapped up in the

112

joke. By the time the punch line came along, I was laughing so hard, I was crying!

I realized after the joke was over that the weight of the world seemed to be lifted from my shoulders. The rest of the afternoon went smoothly and well. One of my positive thoughts had returned and totally turned my day around. How many positive thoughts do you have out in the Universe that have not returned to you?

Do we have to filter positive energy? Yes, we do. The thought was ours. But now, what can our "bodies" expect when we filter this positive energy? (See illustration 14)

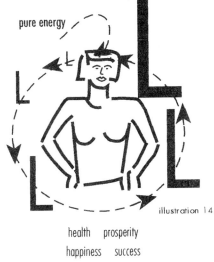

pure energy

illustration 14

health   prosperity

happiness   success

ABUNDANCE IN ALL THINGS

Hopefully you now thoroughly understand how YOUR thoughts <u>have an effect and affect</u> you. You are the creator of your thoughts, whether your thoughts are negative or positive. You are the creator of your life. No one else is responsible for where you are or who you are. (Gee, I think I have said that before. Must be important, huh?)

Back to the question I asked you before. How many negative thoughts do you have out in the universe? They are coming back to you. Can you stop them from returning to you? No, but you can change the negative vibration to a positive vibration.

Would you like to know how to change the negative vibration to a positive vibration? Use the following exercise in the morning, evening, and several times during the day when your schedule will allow. (It only takes a few seconds to use.)

WHITE LIGHT EXERCISE

1. Close your eyes.
2. Take several deep breaths to relax the body.
3. Imagine yourself standing in front of full length dressing mirror. Imagine seeing your reflection.
4. Pretend, imagine, or make believe that you can see White Light coming down from the Universe through the top of your head.
5. The White Light continues down your body, thorough your throat, shoulders, arms and hands, chest, stomach, abdomen, thighs, calves and feet.
6. This White Light fills every cell of your body.
7. Imagine or visualize yourself literally glowing with White Light.
8. Visualize the White Light going back up the body and exiting your body from the center of your forehead, or what some people call the Third Eye.
9. As the White Light exits the Third Eye, visualize it totally surrounding your body, like a mist or a fog.
10. The diameter of the White Light can be as large as YOU want it to be.

WHITE LIGHT exits the THIRD EYE

illustration 15

White Light has the highest energy frequency and is considered by many philosophies to be for protection, perfection, and purity.

I use White Light to fill and surround everything I care about, such as my home, car, loved ones, pets, and myself. The best thing about White Light is the more you use, the better it is!

114

When negative energy is filtered through the White Light, it changes the energy vibrations. All those negative thoughts you still have out in the Universe will be changed into positive energy if you use the White Light.

White Light works for me and many people I know. Remember, you can accept or reject any idea presented in this book, but I hope you will choose to use the White Light.

The knowledge of the White Light DOES NOT give you the right, however, to continue sending out negative energy. If you are a negative person and choose to continue to be a negative person, you will not (in all probability) use the White Light, because it requires time, energy, effort, practice, and a belief in self to control and direct your life.

One of the best reasons to use White Light is that it works whether you believe in it or not. But, for White Light to work, you must use it. I hope you choose to protect yourself with White Light.

THE KEYS TO SUCCESS

In the previous chapters I have given you the tools for becoming a successful human being. I will now give you the keys to unlock those tools. The keys are:

1. Desire
2. Belief
3. Expectation

What are the words that make up the definition of desire, the first key to success?

1. DESIRE is a - **a**. need **b**. want **c**. hope **d**. wish

Of the four mentioned above, which word is the most important to us as a human being, that we have to satisfy first for our survival? Which word has the most energy? A "need", of course! What is it that we need in life to survive as a human being?

1. Air
2. Water
3. Food
4. Clothing
5. Shelter

Think about it. What is the first thing you do with your paycheck? You pay the rent, go grocery shopping, pay your utilities, and buy needed clothes (so far, the government hasn't figured out a way to charge us for air!).

What is a "want"? Let me use an example. If you walk five miles to work in the morning and walk five miles home in the evening, WHAT DO YOU WANT? Personally, I want a car. I do not "need" a car to survive, but a car sure would make my life easier. A "want" has the second highest energy level or priority for us.

In the terms of energy that most people would give to the last two words in desire, I believe "hope" should be number three. Why? Because I can hope for many things and have faith that I will eventually attain these things. I think of these things I "hope" for many times and perhaps shape my life in that direction to attain the things I "hope" for.

When I think of something I would "wish" for, I do not believe I can easily attain it, such as winning a state lottery. It is a "pie in the sky" thought. I do not give the "wish" thought any energy other than a "Wow, what I couldn't do with that money if I won the lottery." I devote about 5 seconds to it.

Let me share another story with you to illustrate a desire.

Socrates was talking with one of his students one day and the student's greatest desire was enlightenment. Socrates told the student that if he desired enlightenment that it should be his. Socrates then turned and walked away. The student was perplexed by Socrates's answer. For weeks after the student had his conversation with his master he studied, read, talked with other people, and did everything he knew to do to become enlightened. Nothing seemed to help him. The next day he saw his master. He walked up to him and said, "Master, Master, I have done everything I know to do to become enlightened, but I have failed in every attempt. Please help me." Socrates turned to the student and told him to come with him. They walked out of the city and down a country lane. Soon they were walking beside a river. Socrates sat down and told his student to sit down beside him. When the student had obeyed, Socrates told him to bend over and look at his reflection in the water. The student followed the instruction. While the student was looking at his reflection in the water, Socrates put his hand on the young man's head and pushed his head under the water. This startled the young man, but he was not afraid. He knew that his master would not hurt him. One minute went by. The student was a little concerned, but he reassured himself that his master would not hurt him. Two minutes went by. He was becoming a "little more concerned", but again he reassured himself that his master would not hurt him. Three minutes went by, and he began to struggle. He was running out of oxygen! On his last struggle, Socrates pulled his head out of the water. The young man was gasping, doing his best to replenish his system with oxygen. Water was running down his face. His hair was in his eyes. When he was finally able to breathe and talk he said, "Master, Master, why did you do that?" Socrates replied, "When I held your head under the water, what was it that you desired most in life?" The student replied, "Why, air of course, Master, air!" Socrates replied, "When you desire enlightenment as much as you desired that air, then it shall be yours."

How much DO YOU desire whatever it is you want in life? How much energy do you give your desire? When you give the amount of energy to your desires as you would to having oxygen to breathe, whatever you desire shall be yours.

What are the ideas that compose the word belief, the second key to success?

2. BELIEF is a - **a.** Conviction
b. deserve to have
c. trusting in self

Which of these ideas has the strongest energy? Which should be number one in the order of importance? A conviction. A "conviction" is our desire, which is a need, want, hope, or wish. The next question is, do I feel I deserve to have whatever it is I need, want, hope, or wish for? This is the part of belief that usually keeps us from what it is we desire in life. It is a limitation that we have accepted from others, usually in childhood. For example:

1. If you don't get a degree, you will never amount to anything.
2. If you are born poor, you will always be poor.
3. The rich keep getting richer, and the poor keep getting poorer.
4. A woman will never hold the same position as a man.
5. A woman's place is in the home.
6. Because I am of a different race I will never...

There are many limitations such as these, a feeling that we "do not deserve to have" that can sabotage us as adults without our realizing why we are unsuccessful. Sometimes we almost make a success at whatever we want, and then something comes along to destroy that success.

If you have not succeeded in life, perhaps you might take a serious look at this particular one. Thank the Universe that a lot of these limitations are being ignored today.

Throughout this book, I hope you have come to the conclusion that to succeed in life, you must trust in yourself, to rely on yourself. It is no one's responsibility to give you what you want in life. But trusting in self depends on your feeling that you deserve to have whatever you desire in life!

Here is story to illustrate belief:

There is a little boy, about six years old, who lives out in the country. The closest neighbors are fifty miles away. His parents land has mountains at the back of his home. He is an only child, and when his parents leave to work the land, he must find ways to entertain himself. One morning after breakfast, he goes out the kitchen door. He is unable to think of anything to do. While he is looking down, he sees a rock that is just the right size to kick. He begins kicking the rock, not paying any attention to where he is going. He crosses a path which leads up the side of the mountain behind his house and proceeds to kick the rock up this path. Hours later he realizes that he is at the top of the mountain. Suddenly, he discovers that he is hungry. He looks up at the sun and realizes that it is getting late. (As we all know, do little boys ever get in a hurry?) The little boy turns around and starts going back down the path, kicking his rock for something to do on his trip down the mountain. The little boy not paying attention to how close he was getting to the edge of the path, his foot slips, and he falls off the side of the mountain. It is almost a sheer drop where he has fallen off, but there is one tree root sticking out of the mountain that the little boy grabs onto. He is frightened, but he keeps his wits about him. He immediately starts looking for other handholds and footholds so he can climb back to the top. There are none that he can see. He begins to think about calling out, hoping someone will hear him, but he remembers that he saw no one coming up the path, nor did he see anyone when he was coming down the path. His little arms are beginning to become tired. Out of desperation, he calls out, "Help, help, is there anybody up there who can help me?" All of a sudden beside him appears his Guardian Angel. She says, "Yes my son, I can help you." The little boy looks at her with disbelief written all over his face. He looks at her, then below her, and replies, "How can you help me?" She says, "I will fly down to the bottom of this mountain. When I call your name, I want you to let go and I will catch you in my arms." The little boy looked at her as if she were crazy! He again starts looking for footholds and handholds, hoping beyond hope that he missed seeing some. He didn't miss any. There were none. He looks back over, and she is still by his side. Again he asks her how she can help him, and she says, "I will fly down to the bottom of this mountain. When I call your name, let go and I will catch you in my arms." The little boy looks away and up to the top of the mountain and yells, "Help, help, is there anybody else up there who can help me?"

120

Belief: how much do you believe in whatever you desire - need, want, hope, or wish for - in life?

The third key to success is expectation. I have known people who desire and believe strongly in what they want in life but never expect to receive it. What is expectation?

3. EXPECTATION IS: **a.** acting as if you have "it" (your desire)

                                    b. acting as if "it" has happened

                                    c. acting as if "it" will happen

What are the verb tenses and the order in which I have used them?

1. Present
2. Past
3. Future

Here is another story that illustrates expectation:

When you leave work today, you are going to stop by your house to change because you are going to attend my seminar. You discovered that sometime during the day, your refrigerator has gone kaput! Just what you needed, right? Well, you have to have a refrigerator, so you take your handy dandy charge card and go to Sears. You walk into the appliance department and pick out your new refrigerator. You give the man your charge card. He writes up the receipt and tells you that your new refrigerator will be delivered Monday afternoon at 4 o'clock. (This is Friday night.) You leave Sears and go to your seminar.

Referring to number one, which is present tense, even though you do not have your refrigerator in your physical presence, (it is to be delivered Monday) aren't you acting as if you already have it? You bought and paid for it; it is yours.

Referring to number two, which is past tense, aren't you acting as if the buying of the refrigerator is in the past, which it is?

Let's continue with the story.

Now while you are at your seminar and all weekend long, what have to been expecting to happen Monday afternoon? (Future tense) Since this is an imaginary story, let's pretend that it is Monday afternoon, 4 o'clock. The Sears truck pulls up outside your house. Two men get out of the truck and go to the back. They open up the doors to the truck.

What are you expecting to come out of the truck? A refrigerator, naturally. Why not a living room suite? Because

121

that is not what you bought and paid for. You paid for a refrigerator! This is how expectation works.

Remember, in a previous chapter I quoted from a very famous book. The
quote was, "Ask, and ye shall receive." This is how your keys function. Desire is
asking for what you want. Believe in that desire once you have sent it out into the
Universe, and the receiving of that desire depends on your expectation. You must
have all three: desire, belief, and expectation, to achieve success. Desire, belief,
and expectation are like a recipe. Leave out one ingredient in the recipe and it
doesn't work.
What is the Largest key of all to accomplishing desire, belief, and
expectation?

__The strength or intensity of energy you give to each one.__

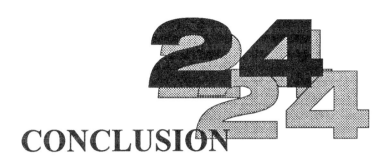

CONCLUSION

With practice you can change your life. You deserve to have whatever you want in life. But remember, nothing you get in life is **FREE**. You must invest your time, energy, effort, and practice into whatever you desire in life. This book gives you the tools, the keys, and the opportunity to accomplish your Goals.

I want you to achieve success in everything you want from life. I want you to be the very "best person" you can be. Your age has nothing to do with your ACHIEVING success. Your station in life has nothing to do with your ACHIEV-ING success. How you THINK does have EVERYTHING to do with ACHIEV-ING your success.

You can use your "Goal Room" to achieve anything you desire in life. Desiring whatever you want in life, believing that you deserve to have your goals in life, and then expecting your goals to become a reality; these are your keys to success. Put the tools you have been given to use by **practicing daily**.

You can acquire all the knowledge in the world, but until you USE that knowledge, that knowledge just "sits in your brain gathering dust", becoming useless information and taking up valuable space. Which person are you going to become, the person you desire or are you going to stay the person you are today?

If you are already successful in many areas of your life (which I am sure many of you are) but are not successful in other areas, you can become more successful by using the tools and keys I have shared with you.

Remember, this is YOUR **"User-Friendly Owner's Manual".** This was written for beginners to start you on the road to success NOW.

I have had a marvelous time writing this book and sharing parts of my life with you. I am sad that the book is ending. I know and understand now what "a labor of love" is. I feel as if I personally know everyone of you because I have been speaking "just to you".

My intentions were to help you start the process of changing your life in an easy, joyful, and fun manner. There are many good books on the market that can give you all the "whys" and "wherefores" of how you came to be the way you are. Read them! BUT, I am a firm believer in making my life what I want it to be NOW. (You know, the "GOD GRANT ME PATIENCE, NOW," syndrome!) I have done my very best to give you the tools and the keys to help you accomplish the changes in your life NOW.

In a few months there will be a workbook to help you further pinpoint the changes you may need to make in your life. You can write or phone the publisher to obtain a release date and where you may obtain a copy.

Remember, no matter what happens in your life, you have one person that believes in and cares about you. That person is me. I wish you many, many successes.

I KNOW you can do it!